"With remarkable detail, corroborating science, and content vetted by a therapist, Shahida unravels the mystery of why so many highly sensitive people are vulnerable to the machinations of persons of disturbed character. A must-read for those looking to reclaim their lives and fulfill their true potential."

—**George Simon, PhD**, author of *In Sheep's Clothing, Character Disturbance, How Did We End Up Here,* and *The Judas Syndrome*

"Outstanding work! Once again, Shahida masterfully blends her own insight and wisdom with evidence-based research and practical strategies for empowering survivors to heal from narcissistic abuse, and effectively disentangle themselves from toxic encounters with individuals that meet criteria for narcissistic or antisocial personality disorders. I regularly recommend Shahida's books to clients in my private practice, and without exception, they emphatically find her writings personally beneficial in multifaceted ways."

—**Athena Staik, PhD**, licensed marriage and family therapist; and author of *What a Narcissist Means When He Says "I Love You"* on her www.psychcentral.com blog, *Neuroscience and Relationships with Dr. Athena Staik*

"Another invaluable recovery resource from Shahida Arabi. This book exposes new types of toxic personalities, offers practical advice for protecting yourself, and dives into the hidden strengths that so many survivors share. An essential guide that teaches us how to empower our empathy."

—**Jackson MacKenzie**, author of *Psychopath Free* and *Whole Again*

"Shahida has become the voice of our generation, a global expert, and a fearless thought leader.

In this book, she not only illuminates the highly sensitive person (HSP) experience, she invites you to nurture your authentic self and discover how to use your 'superpowers' to thrive! If you are sensitive, intuitive, and attuned to the emotions and energy of others, you'll learn not only how to become wonderfully emotionally intelligent, but also how to change your life and our world for the better."

—**Monica M. White, LMHC**, licensed mental health counselor

"I'm a big Shahida fan. Her writing is thoroughly researched, cited, and written in a way that is engaging, witty, and oh-so knowledgeable. This book will help the beginner just realizing what narcissistic abuse is, as well as anyone fully educated and aware. I highly recommend this to therapists, lawyers, judges, and survivors."

—**Kristin Sunanta Walker**, founder of Mental Health News Radio (MHNR) Network: the world's first podcast network dedicated to mental health, with over twelve million listeners

"A must-read for HSPs and for anyone who has ever struggled to understand, handle, and survive toxic people. Shahida has written a book that provides all the answers and information you could ever need in a wonderfully clear, relatable way. This is a book that I wish I had when I was trying to find my way through the minefield of being around toxic people. It will, surely, change lives."

—**Annie Kaszina, PhD**, emotional abuse recovery specialist, and author of *Married to Mr. Nasty*

the highly sensitive person's guide to dealing with toxic people

How to RECLAIM YOUR POWER from NARCISSISTS and OTHER MANIPULATORS

SHAHIDA ARABI, MA

New Harbinger Publications, Inc.

Publisher's Note

NEW HARBINGER PUBLICATIONS is a registered trademark of New Harbinger Publications, Inc.

Distributed in Canada by Raincoast Books

Copyright © 2020 by Shahida Arabi
New Harbinger Publications, Inc.
5674 Shattuck Avenue
Oakland, CA 94609
www.newharbinger.com

Cover design by Amy Daniel

Acquired by Jess O'Brien

Edited by Cindy Nixon

All Rights Reserved

Library of Congress Cataloging-in-Publication Data

Names: Arabi, Shahida, author.
Title: The highly sensitive person's guide to dealing with toxic people: how to reclaim your power from narcissists and other manipulators / Shahida Arabi.
Description: Oakland, CA: New Harbinger Publications, Inc., [2020] | Includes bibliographical references.
Identifiers: LCCN 2020012135 (print) | LCCN 2020012136 (ebook) | ISBN 9781684035304 (trade paperback) | ISBN 9781684035311 (pdf) | ISBN 9781684035328 (epub)
Subjects: LCSH: Interpersonal conflict. | Psychological abuse. | Manipulative behavior.
Classification: LCC BF637.I48 A73 2020 (print) | LCC BF637.I48 (ebook) | DDC 158.2--dc23
LC record available at https://lccn.loc.gov/2020012135
LC ebook record available at https://lccn.loc.gov/2020012136

Printed in the United States of America

24	23	22			
10	9	8	7	6	5

Contents

Foreword

Dear Reader,

It is a great honor and privilege to write the foreword for Shahida Arabi's new book. Over the last five years, I've been fortunate to work with Shahida in the field of narcissistic abuse recovery. As a licensed clinical therapist, I have referred clients to her exceptional writing on numerous occasions, as well as her informative and supportive website, to help provide them with validation, research-based tools, and suggestions for recovery.

In this book, Shahida blends research with tangible and practical solutions for empowerment and healing in such a way that is readable, interesting, and applicable. She crafts a medicinal alchemy of fact, compassion, and experiential strategies for survivors of relationship abuse and those encountering toxic people at all points along the toxicity spectrum. If you have been looking for effective approaches to the toxic people in your life, from the benign to the malignant, look no further. You have come to the right place, as the pages that follow are chock-full of evidence-based and strengths-focused nuggets of wisdom. You will also be treated to outstanding recommendations for easy-to-implement strategies on subjects such as boundary-setting, healing modalities, self-care, and coping skills when confronted with toxic people in intimate partner relationships.

Shahida's latest contribution to the field helps highly sensitive people dismantle the effects of addictive abuse cycles and overcome relationship trauma by providing in-depth information and insight about the tactics of psychological abuse, the effects of relational trauma on our brains, and specific strategies on how to best tackle manipulative people. Shahida also beautifully weaves in journaling reflections and exercises throughout the book to further reinforce a survivor's newly honed knowledge and apply innovative approaches to healing.

No doubt you have researched numerous articles and scoured websites to find answers to your questions about narcissistic abuse, highly sensitive persons (HSPs), empaths, narcissists, psychopaths, and emotional abuse. HSPs and empaths form a unique and compassionate group of people who are frequently the target of relationship abuse. In this book, Shahida provides a comprehensive analysis of the dynamic between HSPs and toxic people, along with practical ways to create a psychological shield of protection in recovery. She empowers HSPs to tap into their innate "superpowers" and gifts, which can be true assets in discerning healthy relationships and boundary-setting as healing ensues. I can't think of a more helpful book to recommend to highly sensitive people who want to better understand themselves, know what hit them, learn how to heal, and discover how to move forward into thriving.

My clients in private practice resoundingly state that they appreciate Shahida's wonderful writings, as her style is truly strengths-focused and evidence-based. She knows exactly what a survivor is experiencing and how painful narcissistic abuse recovery can be, which is what allows her work to reach readers in an empathic way while also grounding them firmly in the reality of toxic people and narcissists. She is profoundly aware that survivors often internalize the shame that has been projected upon them from the abuser's gaslighting, blame-shifting, and other emotional abuse tactics. She knows they are struggling with the aftermath of the addictive cycle that often develops with manipulators. With that, Shahida works in earnest to express sound, clinically relevant strategies for healing in a nurturing, compassionate manner. Her book reads like a wise friend comforting wounded kindred spirits on the journey of recovery from relationship trauma.

Shahida is, without a doubt, one of the most informed voices on the subject of healing in the wake of intimate partner abuse, specifically psychological abuse. Furthermore, she is an exceptionally authentic life coach, researcher, and author, a person of integrity who practices what she preaches and is an outstanding example to her readers. She knows what works based upon her research and outreach with the survivor population. She bravely and transparently shares her healing suggestions, grounded in research, personal life experiences, and consultation with other experts in the field.

So, dear reader, grab a cup of warm tea, start a fire in the fireplace, and nuzzle up on your couch with this book. Enjoy this wonderful contribution to the field of psychological abuse recovery and highly sensitive people. Healing awaits you as you learn more about the next steps in your transformation into a fully empowered highly sensitive person.

—Andrea Schneider, MSW, LCSW

The Highly Sensitive Person's Journey Among Toxic People

When my article "20 Diversion Tactics Highly Manipulative Narcissists, Sociopaths, and Psychopaths Use to Silence You" went viral in 2016, it reached over eighteen million people all over the world. Survivors of narcissistic individuals and mental health professionals alike shared the article with the fervor of recognition. People were astounded to see the manipulation tactics they had experienced firsthand laid out for them, and many commented that I must have known their narcissistic ex-spouse, sibling, parent, or coworker. I received many letters telling me that I had captured something that people had been trying to find validation for and understanding of for years.

Highly sensitive persons (HSPs) are in a unique position to encounter a wide variety of toxic people, because manipulators look for people with empathy, conscientiousness, and emotional responsiveness to exploit. Many who reached out to me experienced the high end of the toxicity spectrum, such as narcissistic, sociopathic, and psychopathic individuals. These victims:

- Had encountered toxic and narcissistic individuals in their relationships, friendships, the workplace, and even within their own families

- Were idealized, devalued, sabotaged, and inevitably discarded by these toxic types in ways that were cruel and callous

- Suffered months, years, even decades of verbal, emotional, and sometimes even physical or sexual abuse designed to psychologically torment and destroy them

- Were isolated, coerced, belittled, and controlled by their partners behind closed doors

- Endured stalking, harassment, pathological envy, rage attacks, chronic infidelity, and pathological lying

- Were targeted by elaborate schemes and scams that undermined them and drained them of their resources

As a self-help author, I've corresponded with thousands of survivors of toxic people. I've learned that toxic people and narcissists find it quite easy to convince a highly empathic and conscientious person that they are paranoid, losing it, or just "overreacting" when being manipulated. Therefore, these are the people who are targeted, because they can be conditioned to doubt themselves.

It's very likely that if you're reading this book, you can relate to feeling overwhelmed by the toxic people around you. Whether it's an overbearing coworker who constantly criticizes you or an abusive partner who belittles you daily, toxic people can take a toll on the mind, body, and spirit. More "benign" manipulators may cause inconvenience, stress, annoyance, and overall dissatisfaction, and they may occasionally use silencing tactics. More "malignant" manipulators, however, such as narcissists who lack empathy, pose serious harm and risk to your health, well-being, and even your life, using manipulation tactics as a primary mode of interacting with the world. Malignant manipulators exhibit hardwired behaviors that are unlikely to change, whereas benign manipulators may be more receptive to changing and boundary-setting. Though there is a spectrum of toxicity, being prepared for all the shades toxicity can come in is an essential life skill for HSPs to learn.

The survivors who have written to me are highly sensitive and empathic humans. They've been told their entire lives that they are "too sensitive." If you think you may be an HSP, the purpose of this book is to help you learn to use your sensitivity to listen to your instincts about these con artists, rather than continually betraying your inner voice.

Since this form of manipulation and abuse is so covert, you may be suffering in silence before you learn to identify what you are experiencing. This is a common side effect of what we know as *gaslighting*—a tactic in toxic relationships where your perception and reality are constantly questioned and invalidated, and you are told that you are imagining things, oversensitive, and blowing things out of proportion despite mounting evidence to the contrary. A survivor, Annie, described to me her dizzying experience of crazy-making conversations with her narcissistic partner. "When we'd get into an argument and I would back up my side with facts, he would take those facts and spin them around in so many circles that by the end of the argument, he was able to use some of those same facts for himself and leave me feeling lost and 'crazy.' I'd walk away asking myself how I ever thought standing up for myself was a good thing to do in the first place."

The effects of such disorienting behavior are meant to keep victims of gaslighting walking on eggshells and doubting themselves. Chris experienced emotional and mental abuse in addition to sexual coercion at the hands of his narcissistic girlfriend. His relationship was rife with gaslighting and mind games, which are all too common in cases of covert abuse. He said, "It led me to question my instincts and sanity. She was spinning me around with conflicting stories and discounting evidence that my beliefs were valid. She tried to force me into sexual acts I was not comfortable with and shame me when I didn't comply."

Gaslighting can be extreme when it is used to paint the true abuser as victim, which often happens in cases of abuse. When a toxic person cannot control you, they often resort to controlling the conversation about you by slandering you and staging smear campaigns. Another survivor, Molly, shared with me her harrowing story of how her narcissistic partner tried to stage his own death to frame her and spread lies about her sanity. She wrote: "He held a gun to his head and said that he'd kill himself, make it look like murder to ensure I was to blame if I didn't shoot myself after. He'd tell his family and our close friends that we had true love, yet behind my back tell them I was crazy and suicidal—and he was doing the best he could to help me. I have never been suicidal. This all caused my closest friends and family to lose all faith in me and he totally secluded me from the outside world, limiting me to one meal a day while nursing our newborn."

Although toxicity exists on a spectrum, the merciless cruelty of these individuals cannot be underestimated, particularly when they lack empathy, as narcissists do. These are not normal relationship problems or indicative of a "communication" problem—these are patterns of heinous abuse and calculated mind games. I've heard countless tales of narcissistic individuals retaliating against their victims, especially when their victims decide to leave them—everything from stalking and harassing their victims to releasing their intimate photos and even trying to smear them in their place of work. For example, more than a few victims have told me their toxic partners attempted to paint them as drug addicts to their employers.

I've also been privy to numerous horrific incidents of toxic people abandoning their loved ones in times of distress, grief, pregnancy, miscarriage, and even life-threatening illness. As Tracy, a survivor, described, "I found out that the tissue the doctor removed was an aggressive, unpredictable form of cancer, that I needed to have it removed and it could return or migrate to other tissue or organs. I told him later that same night at dinner at a restaurant. His reply? 'Are we going to talk about this cancer thing all night?' The morning after my surgery, I asked him if he could make me some coffee and he asked me in return, 'Why can't you do it yourself?'"

To normal, empathic people, this type of ruthlessness is unprecedented and unbelievable. To a narcissist, this is a way of life. The farther someone is on the spectrum of toxicity, the more sadistic and deliberately malicious they can be. As another survivor, Pauline, recounted, "He told me, 'If I don't make you cry every year on your birthday, I haven't done my job.' He wasn't talking about happy tears. I found him in bed with a bridesmaid at a friend's wedding reception at the hotel after-party. I opened our hotel room door to find them together, and he asked me, 'Do you want to be in the middle, or should I?'"

Some of us have encountered toxic people in our own families or were raised by one. One survivor, Damiana, described how her narcissistic mother discarded her during times of illness. "She went out all day. My father found me having fainted and immersed in my vomit. I was dying from peritonitis and I had surgery in the ER. I spent one week in the hospital. My mother came to visit me just two or three times and she never apologized for leaving me alone. The second time, I was twelve. I had the chicken pox, I didn't feel well, but my mother prevented me from resting at home. The first day of illness she went in my bedroom yelling like crazy at me: 'Out of this house! I don't want to see you!' I had to spend my days out in the street, with my skin full of itchy scabs. With shame and embarrassment."

The impact of toxic parenting can have lifelong effects on victims. Amanda, who grew up with a physically abusive narcissistic father, told me she still suffered as an adult from the impact of having such a malignant parent. She described how she perpetually panicked about whether she had made the right decision and often looked to others to validate her perceptions and actions. She said, "I constantly second-guess my evaluation of situations, and my responses to them. I can't seem to trust my own sense of reality." It was only when she finally had a "name" for her father's behavior that she began to understand and heal from her trauma. "I always felt that there was just something intrinsically wrong with me, but it was him all along," she concluded.

This type of second-guessing is very common among adult children of narcissistic parents as well as survivors of an abusive relationship with a narcissist. As I learned from surveying 733 adult children of narcissistic parents for a previous book, not only does chronic gaslighting instill a persistent sense of self-doubt, but it also leaves the survivor with a shaky sense of self-worth in adulthood. Adult children of narcissists feel "defective" because they experience these traumas at a vulnerable young age. As a result, they suffer from toxic shame and self-blame, self-harm, addiction, suicidal ideation, and a pattern of getting involved with narcissists in adulthood.

Friendships, too, can be rife with narcissistic abuse. Narcissistic friends often target individuals they feel most threatened by or are envious of. Much like the dynamic in relationships, I've heard many stories of how narcissistic friends first flatter and charm HSPs to gain their trust, only to sabotage them and taint their reputation later. One survivor recounted the abrupt betrayal of a good friend who, although first appearing to be amicable and warm, later openly pursued her boyfriend with unprecedented sadism. As she said, "She took pride in the ability to destroy my relationship while appearing to advance herself above me. She made a point to make this drama public and to put me down in front of our mutual social circle." The impact of such a betrayal, combined with calculated slander, was so overwhelming for her that she suffered hypertension, a loss of appetite, and depression. "It was an early learning experience on just how cruel a person could be," she told me.

HSPs like you who've been ensnared by toxic predators tend to blame themselves and look within when they come across insidious abuse. After all, we've been taught by society to discount our instincts and to treat our high sensitivity like a problem rather than a potential skill set. So, speaking out against such a manipulator and, ultimately, speaking up for ourselves can feel like a death sentence, especially when the manipulator in question wears such a well-constructed false mask. As survivor Rebecca told me, her ex-husband was a public figure who hid behind the "cloak of righteousness." She said, "I was affected in many ways. I didn't know who I was. I couldn't make choices for myself. I felt helpless and hopeless. I hated myself. I got to a point where I thought I was the crazy one." I have heard countless survivor stories of narcissistic people who managed to convince society that the abuse—in whatever form it took, whether verbal, physical, sexual, financial, or emotional—did not occur at all.

We are further invalidated by court systems, law enforcement, family, friends, and sometimes even our own therapists who do not realize that this is no "normal" breakup or relationship issue—this is a power dynamic that disrupts every aspect of the survivor's life and mental health. Emotional and psychological abuse destroys self-esteem and self-worth, leaving long-lasting, debilitating effects.

What makes this type of abuse even more traumatizing is the inability to find validation of the immense pain experienced. Victims sometimes go to therapy to find ways to deal with this type of abuse only to be misdiagnosed or encouraged to adapt to their abusers instead of exiting the relationship. They can be further gaslighted into believing they are dealing with someone with empathy and the capacity to change. There are also those who have the misfortune of attending couples therapy only to have their narcissistic partner bamboozle the therapist, play the victim, and use the therapy space as a playground for their various schemes.

You see, not all therapists or academics fully understand the dynamics of covert manipulation and abuse by these predatory types. Why would they? Real narcissists and psychopaths don't go to therapy unless court-ordered to do so, and many wear a compelling false mask. Toxic people live in denial and entitlement, and they feel rewarded by their exploitative behavior. The nature of their disordered behavior is often uniquely hidden behind closed doors, so in order to heal, you would need validation from survivors and trauma-informed therapists who truly "get it."

Like these survivors, and possibly you, I have intimate knowledge of how toxic people operate and what it's like to navigate the world as an HSP. Growing up severely bullied by peers and witnessing emotional abuse were the catalysts that drove me to a lifelong journey of extreme self-care. My high sensitivity and empathy made me a vulnerable target for a variety of toxic people. My childhood programming conditioned me to have friendships and relationships with narcissistic individuals who lacked empathy. Like many survivors of narcissists, I also became entangled in toxic work environments. Learning to adapt to, cope with, and ultimately exit these types of situations while remaining true to myself challenged me to grow in ways I otherwise would not have.

I know firsthand and from speaking to survivors that healing from the devastation these toxic types cause takes enormous inner work. By the tender age of twenty, I was practicing daily meditation, doing all types of yoga, and experimenting with cognitive behavioral therapy, eye movement desensitization and reprocessing, emotional freedom techniques, and dialectical behavior therapy as potential modes of healing. I read hundreds of self-help books and took graduate courses in psychology, psychopathology, and sociology at New York University, Columbia University, and Harvard University. I researched bullying and surveyed thousands of survivors just like me for my books. For my master's thesis at Columbia University, I interviewed bully victims, some of whom later became targets for narcissistic dating partners. As a result of all these experiences, I gained a deep understanding and solid knowledge base about the tactics toxic people use and how to navigate them effectively across various contexts.

You've probably found that interactions with toxic people have given you skill sets and knowledge you did not possess prior. Like many children who survive a war zone, as an adult I could recognize toxicity with a far more discerning eye than most. I learned there was a spectrum. While some toxic people are unintentionally toxic, others are deliberately malicious. While a handful are able to change with hard work and brutal self-reflection, most remain cunning and aggressive. HSPs such as myself have to swallow these uncomfortable truths in order to understand the mind-set of someone who seeks to harm us.

If you're an HSP, you've probably developed a destructive habit over the years of trying to educate toxic people on how to be more empathic or considerate. You've probably struggled with boundaries and with extricating yourself from toxic people. This book is meant to help you curb harmful habits like these and refocus on your own self-care, boundaries, and self-protection. In this book, I've integrated life lessons and wisdom not only from my own life but also from the insights I've accumulated from the thousands of survivors and the many experts I've communicated with in order to formulate reasonable advice to better handle these toxic types.

As you work on building healthy boundaries, you will gradually realize it is not your job or responsibility to fix anyone or teach them basic human decency. You are not their parent or therapist—and you've no doubt been quite generous with people who didn't deserve your efforts to help. Spend that time instead on considering whether these people are worthy of being in your life and detaching rather than feeding into the attachment by trying to "change" them. They are adults, and they can change themselves on their own.

This book is not a substitution for therapy; although it was vetted by a licensed clinician, it is meant only as a self-help guide. You should always consider therapy with a licensed professional if you are healing from trauma, have doubts about putting any of these suggestions into practice, or have concerns about your safety. These self-care tips are meant only to supplement your journey toward greater self-esteem, healing, and boundary implementation. Take what works for you and adapt it to your personal circumstances. My hope is that with the information in this book, you will not only learn to make use of the gift that is your high sensitivity but also become highly strategic in your navigation of toxic people.

If you've realized you're an HSP with a habit of becoming entangled with toxic people, know that you're not alone. While some of the traits that make you an HSP can leave you vulnerable to emotional predators, you also have traits that can be used as strengths to detect toxic people, establish solid boundaries, and tackle their manipulation head-on.

Society might have taught you that your sensitivity is a weakness, but it can be your biggest strength. Your "extra" sensitivity is your inner alarm system and shield. It goes off more quickly in the presence of danger. The trick is to tune in to your sensitivity and listen to your inner voice. As an empathic human being, your sensitivity is a superpower. You will learn in the next few chapters exactly how to use this superpower to better distinguish among the different types of toxic people and how to navigate these relationships in ways that best cater to your high sensitivity and self-care needs.

CHAPTER ONE

The Trinity
HSPs, Toxic Manipulators, and Narcissists

Do you go through each day with overwhelming and intense emotions? You feel like an emotional sponge, constantly taking on the moods and states of others. When you are interacting with someone, you absorb everything: you're highly attuned to changes in their facial expression, their slight shifts in tone of voice, and their nonverbal gestures. Criticism and conflict have devastating effects on you and have the potential to ruin your entire day. Large crowds drain you, bright lights unsettle you, and rough textures and strong scents agitate you. You often find yourself in relationships with toxic people or even being taken advantage of by narcissists. Chances are high that because you are reading this book, this is your reality and you may be what psychology researchers refer to as a *highly sensitive person (HSP)*.

You may have always felt different than others—you *feel* more and you experience the world more vividly and more deeply, almost as if you're encountering the world on a higher volume. As Elena Herdieckeroff (2016) describes in her TED Talk on highly sensitive people, "All of your senses [are] on high alert … all of your emotions are magnified. A sadness is a deep sorrow and a joy is pure ecstasy. You also care beyond reason and empathize without limits. Imagine being in permanent osmosis with everything around you." This isn't the result of a quirky personality; it's the blessing and the curse of an actual genetic trait. High sensitivity is a genetic proclivity that allows us to process stimuli more thoroughly, pick up on subtleties in our environment, and have more vivid perceptions of negative and positive experiences.

If you are highly sensitive, you are not alone, even though you may feel like it. According to researcher Elaine Aron, HSPs constitute 15 to 20 percent of the population (2016, xxv). An HSP or someone with sensory processing sensitivity is more emotionally and physically responsive to the self, to their environment, and to their relationships with others. As an HSP, you have a highly tuned radar for everything happening around you. This trait makes you more prone to overstimulation, but it can also come with the many benefits of being extremely discerning in your interactions with others—once you learn to tune in to your heightened perceptions.

The high sensitivity we possess makes us more vulnerable to toxic people. This is because HSPs, along with the closely related group of people who are more colloquially termed "empaths," can easily take on the emotions of others as our own. Since we have porous boundaries, we end up taking on the pain and stress of others, absorbing negativity more frequently from others in our day-to-day life, more so than the average person. Due to our ability to be overly conscientious, empathic, and attuned to the needs of others, HSPs can easily become ensnared in the web of toxic people. Before diving deep into that dynamic, let's further explore the trait of high sensitivity. Understanding yourself better will help you more accurately perceive what's going on and also begin to pave a path toward living healthily as an HSP.

The Science Behind High Sensitivity

High sensitivity is not just a feeling—it's a scientific fact. In a study conducted by Bianca Acevedo and colleagues (2014), fMRI scans revealed that the brains of HSPs reacted more strongly to emotionally evocative pictures. The brain regions related to awareness, empathy, integration of sensory information, reward processing, and even action-oriented planning were more highly activated in HSPs than in their less sensitive peers when viewing the facial expressions of both strangers and partners. This could explain why we as HSPs tend to be more responsive to social situations and the emotions of others than most people. Here's more of the science that explains why we respond the way we do.

Why We Feel More: Empathy and Mirror Neurons

Have you ever wondered if there's a reason you are more emotionally responsive and empathic to the pain of others—going so far as to feel their pain like your own? Why seeing someone harmed affects you more deeply than it does your peers? Why you have a tendency to try to "fix," rescue, and heal people? There is a biological reason in the form of our enhanced *mirror neurons*, a type of sensory-motor brain cell that fires in the same way as another person's when we observe that person performing an action, almost as if we were performing that action ourselves, even if we haven't moved a muscle (Marsh and Ramachandran 2012).

As you learned earlier, research confirms that areas of the brain with the greatest activity in HSPs include the mirror neuron system, which is associated with our empathetic responses, awareness, processing of sensory information, and action planning. As a result, our empathy is more heightened than that of others and we are "sponges" for the emotions of others. In addition, HSPs are more action-oriented and empathic when witnessing the pain of others (Acevedo et al. 2014). Our mirror neuron system enables us to "feel" what another person might be feeling when we see someone doing something, as the same regions in our brain that would have been involved in doing that activity become activated. This heightened mirror neuron system can enhance both positive and negative experiences in social situations (Aron 2016). We can witness someone's pain and feel as if we're experiencing it ourselves, just as much as we can experience their elation at happy news.

For example, watching another person cry can cause us to cry immediately in response because we can feel the weight of their discomfort and suffering. If a loved one tells us of a traumatic event they went through, we can experience a form of secondary trauma. We might envision every single terrible ordeal they went through during that traumatic event and see it in our minds as if we had been there ourselves, experiencing what that person endured. We place ourselves in their shoes vividly.

This form of sensitivity can build connection between two empathic people. It can, however, also result in one-sided, parasitic relationships with toxic people. As HSPs, we often take responsibility for the emotions and issues of others. While this high level of empathy and compulsion to "rescue" can be advantageous when we are called to engage in activism and help populations in need, it actually makes us even more vulnerable to toxic people who seek our sympathy in order to continue their destructive behavior. When we are always swayed by another person's pain, we fail to take into account how they are treating *us*. Instead, we reconcile with them quickly, rationalizing their unacceptable behavior. Manipulative people depend on this trait to exploit us, as we'll discuss in more depth later in this chapter.

Enhanced Perception and Attunement to Our Environment

HSPs are not only attuned to other people, but we are also deeply connected to our environment. Research shows that HSPs have more activity in the part of the brain known as the *insula*, leading to a greater depth of processing, attunement to changes in the environment, and enhanced perception of experiences; HSPs also show a heightened awareness of subtle stimuli and are more reactive to both positive and negative stimuli (Jagiellowicz et al. 2011). The insula is responsible for self-awareness and plays an important role in processing bodily sensations that contribute to our decision making. Researcher Bud Craig (2009) says the insula is responsible for what he calls the "global emotional moment" because it collects information about our environment, bodily sensations, and emotions to create a subjective experience of the present moment. HSPs are thought to process their environment and experiences on a far deeper level than most of the population. We are able to recognize and identify patterns, take in information more thoroughly, connect past and present experiences, and think over decisions in a more comprehensive and intuitive manner than non-HSPs.

You might experience a "global emotional moment" when you meet someone new. As you form your overall first impression of them, you take in their nonverbal gestures, facial microexpressions, tone of voice, and emotional state while simultaneously processing your own emotional state, bodily sensations, and details in your environment. You might meet Mary, for instance, who seems charming at the outset, but you pick up on a hint of contempt, a certain haughtiness in the way she carries herself, and a disingenuously sweet tone of voice, along with your own feelings of discomfort and visceral reactions that indicate anxiety.

The problem is, even as an HSP in this situation, you might rationalize away your observations because of Mary's charismatic façade. The trick is learning that your ability to pick up on nuances is an asset, not a drawback, when meeting new people. Your brain's capacity to collect and process massive amounts of information can serve you well in your decision-making process, especially when it comes to weeding out potentially toxic individuals from your life.

This depth of processing can go in two different directions depending on the circumstances: in one situation, HSPs are more likely to weigh the pros and cons before making a decision; in another, they can quickly process when their present situation is very much like a past one and react immediately to any danger it presents. As Elaine Aron writes, "In other words, sensitivity, or responsivity as [it is] also called, involves paying more attention to details than others do, then using that knowledge to make better predictions in the future" (2016, xv). Considering this, as an HSP, you *already* have many of the internal tools at your disposal to assess and discern toxic people accurately. You just need to work on listening to yourself and complement that intuition with the action-based steps I'll share in this book.

How Our Early Childhood Environment Shapes Us

"You're so *sensitive* and touchy," my classmate sneered as I cried on the playground after hearing an insulting comment. Being severely bullied in middle school had a profound impact on me. Not only was I terrorized by my peers, but I was also constantly belittled for reacting to the abuse at all. My emotions were rarely validated.

As an HSP, you've probably been called "too sensitive" since you were a child. You may have also struggled with high levels of anxiety, depression, or even neuroticism. These are not necessarily inherent in the trait of high sensitivity, yet being an HSP can put you at risk for these if you also had *adverse childhood experiences* (ACEs), a term that refers to stressful or traumatic events in childhood, such as physical, sexual, or emotional abuse, physical or emotional neglect, witnessing domestic violence, having a family member with a mental illness or an addiction, parental separation or divorce, witnessing a mother being treated violently, and the incarceration of a family member.

The CDC-Kaiser Permanente Adverse Childhood Experiences study was one of the largest studies conducted on those who had suffered child abuse and neglect (Felitti et al. 1998). It evaluated the effects of the childhood abuse on health and well-being in adulthood. It discovered that those who had suffered a number of ACEs were more at risk for chronic health problems, substance abuse, self-harm, and suicidal ideation.

If your childhood was rife with emotional neglect, abuse, or bullying, your high sensitivity can interact with these experiences to produce these issues in adulthood. "Nurture" interacts with "nature," such that toxic early environments leave highly sensitive types more vulnerable to stress. As Elaine Aron writes, "HSPs with a troubled childhood are more at risk of becoming depressed, anxious, and shy than non-sensitive people with a similar childhood; but those with good-enough childhoods were no more at risk than others" (2016, xi). HSPs also have a genetic variation that leads to having less serotonin in their brains, a phenomenon that is even more pronounced in those with a difficult childhood.

However, this same genetic variation also comes with benefits, including improved memory of learned material, better decision making, and overall better mental functioning. As Aron (2016) notes in her book, rhesus monkeys with this trait were found (if raised by good mothers) to show something known as *developmental precocity*: being leaders of their social groups and having high levels of resilience (Suomi 2011).

As an HSP, even if you had adverse childhood experiences, you have many gifts and abilities that can contribute to the world in positive ways. Your resilience and your ability to pick up on subtleties and nuances others miss are unparalleled. This can work *for* you rather than against you, as long as you learn how to use these abilities skillfully to navigate relationships and conflicts.

JOURNAL REFLECTION: **Adverse Childhood Experiences**
Consider the following questions and record your responses in your journal. Did you have any adverse childhood experiences? How have they affected you in adulthood? Did your high sensitivity influence how you responded? In what ways does it show up?

A Note About Empaths

Although there are skeptics who claim that the term "empath" belongs in the realm of pseudoscience, HSPs are perhaps the closest group we've been able to study scientifically whose abilities overlap with those of empaths. Empaths are said to directly experience the emotions of others. According to Judith Orloff, MD, "Empaths feel things first, *then* think, which is the opposite of how most people function in our over-intellectualized society. There is no membrane that separates us from the world" (2018, 5).

The idea that we can take on the emotions of others is not an unscientific one either. Research indicates that *emotional contagion*, the tendency to "catch" the feelings of others, is more common than we think (Hatfield, Cacioppo, and Rapson 2003). Sherrie Bourg Carter (2012) writes, "Studies have found that the mimicry of a frown or a smile or other kinds of emotional expression trigger reactions in our brains that cause us to interpret those expressions as our own feelings. Simply put, as a species, we are innately vulnerable to 'catching' other people's emotions."

HSPs and empaths are deeply intuitive individuals who are highly attuned to the emotions and energy of others. We experience this sense of emotional contagion on a heightened level. While these two terms—"empath" and "HSP"—are distinct, they share many similarities and characteristics. For the HSP, the parts of the brain that regulate emotions are simply more responsive than those of their less sensitive peers. There is great overlap between what it means to be an HSP and what society calls an "empath."

Whether you consider yourself an empath or an HSP, know that while these tips and strategies are tailored toward the overlapping traits between these two groups, I will be using the term "HSP" throughout this book.

The Spectrum of Sensitivity

According to Elaine Aron, since high sensitivity is a genetic trait, you either "are" or you "aren't"—you either have the trait or you don't. However, as alluded to above, psychologists note that nature and nurture work together; biological predisposition usually interacts with environment to produce how that trait is presented. Your high sensitivity interacts with any mental health conditions, traumas, cultural or religious backgrounds, or adverse childhood experiences you have, producing a different expression of your high sensitivity than someone else's.

For example, I am an HSP, but I'm also an HSP who grew up in and currently lives in Manhattan—a hotbed of loud noises, crowds, and bright lights. While I'm inherently sensitive to these factors, I find that I can tolerate this type of intense stimulation more so than most because, as a child, I was raised in very unruly, chaotic environments both at school and at home. As a result of my upbringing, I've gotten accustomed to overstimulating factors and I am able to "tune them out" when desired.

In contrast, another HSP who hails from a small town might have elevated sensitivity to loud noises, crowds, and bright lights because they are not used to such an environment. Nevertheless, if their childhood experiences were peaceful, they will likely be less emotionally responsive to chaotic social situations than someone whose background includes bullying or abuse.

Both types of people "count" as highly sensitive, but our experiences do shape the degrees to which the trait presents itself and how.

EXERCISE: **HSP Checklist**

Go through the following list of social behaviors most commonly associated with HSPs and check off those that apply to you. The more check marks, the greater the likelihood that you're an HSP.

☐ You are more emotionally reactive to situations and people than most individuals are. You're often called "very sensitive."

☐ You are deeply empathic and attuned to the emotional states of others. You become an "emotional sponge" to the moods and feelings of others without realizing it.

☐ You find yourself wanting to help those who are in pain, and you anticipate the emotional needs of others. You go out of your way to make others feel comfortable, especially when they're distressed.

☐ You experience high levels of intuition about people, places, and situations that later turn out to be true.

☐ Regardless of whether you are more extroverted or introverted (around 30 percent of HSPs are extroverted), you require a significant amount of alone time to process experiences and emotions.

☐ Because of your high depth of processing, you pick up on subtleties and nuances others cannot. You are extremely responsive to changes in your environment and the emotions of others. You are adept at reading people beyond surface-level impressions, able to "sense" when someone is lying, note the discrepancies between words and body language, and detect slight shifts in facial microexpressions, tone, or nonverbal gestures others might miss.

☐ You have a rich and vivid inner life, with a massive degree of introspection, creativity, and imagination. You may be drawn to the arts, which move you and evoke an emotional response.

☐ You have a generous nature and keen insights into the human psyche. A natural-born healer, you may gravitate toward professions that incorporate some form of caretaking, leadership, or teaching.

☐ You feel easily overwhelmed by your environment, especially if it contains large crowds, bright lights, loud sounds, and strong scents. You find yourself exiting or wanting to exit environments with these elements or feeling moody in them.

☐ You ruminate over people, decisions, and situations for longer periods of time than most people. For example, you can mull over a critical comment for weeks or take considerably longer than the average person to get over a breakup.

☐ You become easily stimulated by interactions with others. One minute, you might be calm and relaxed. The next, after a social interaction, you find yourself feeling emotionally charged, without always knowing why.

☐ You may struggle with depression, anxiety, and self-doubt due to your high sensitivity and receptiveness to taking on the emotions of others. You might have various addictions to emotionally "numb" yourself to the intensity of the emotions you experience.

☐ You find yourself approached by toxic people who trespass your boundaries on a regular basis—people who drain you and exploit you without giving you much in return.

☐ You've had a series of unhealthy relationships with narcissistic per-sonalities who have used your empathy and sensitivity against you.

Therapy Check-In: Do You Need a Therapist?

Remember that HSPs who come from traumatic backgrounds are at higher risk for anxiety and depression. Their high sensitivity can inter-act with the trauma to produce certain mental health conditions. Regardless of your childhood background, it's important to consult a therapist if you experience **any** of the following:

- Persistently high levels of anxiety or chronic panic attacks

- Extreme social anxiety, resulting in self-isolation

- Flashbacks, intrusive thoughts, or nightmares

- Chronic negative self-talk and self-sabotage

- Dissociation (feeling detached from your body, your environ-ment, or both)

- Suicidal ideation or plans to harm yourself

- Previous incidents of self-harm

- Psychosomatic symptoms and bodily issues that don't seem to have a medical explanation

- Issues with body image and eating disorders

- Experience of a recent traumatic event or secondary trauma by witnessing someone else's trauma

- Addictions or compulsions, including any obsessive-compulsive rituals

- A history of abusive relationships, friendships, or exploitative work environments

- Any form of psychosis (for example, hallucinations, hearing voices)

- Issues with maintaining healthy relationships or attachments to others

Magnets for Toxic People

When HSPs come into contact with toxic individuals who are empathy-impaired or even conscienceless, their minds, bodies, and spirits can become overwhelmed. On one of the largest survivor forums for those affected by narcissistic partners, Psychopath Free, an online poll was taken to see which Myers-Briggs personality types tended to be the victims of narcissistic individuals. Unsurprisingly, the most popular types represented were INFJs and INFPs (to learn more about the Myers-Briggs Type Indicator, see https://www.myersbriggs.org). These personality types are associated with common HSP traits such as emotional intensity, conscientiousness, and a high level of empathy and intuition.

HSPs can be targeted by those on the malignant end of the toxicity spectrum: narcissistic, psychopathic, and sociopathic personalities. But there are also garden-variety toxic personalities who can drain our emotional reserves. As we'll explore later in the book, these personalities are on the lower end of the spectrum of toxicity because they are *usually* unaware of the impact they leave and are capable of reflecting on their actions when confronted, even showing improvement. These personality types consist of what are called "boundary-steppers," "emotional vampires," "crazy-makers," and "attention-seekers."

Overview of the Dangerous Behaviors of Narcissistic Individuals

We'll dive deeper into the distinctions between garden-variety toxic people and malignant narcissists in chapter 2, but for the time being, you should be aware of the terms used to explain narcissistic behaviors. If you see the following behaviors being used on a consistent basis to keep you off-balance, you may be dealing with a dangerous narcissistic individual.

Gaslighting. A person who engages in this behavior denies your perception of reality and minimizes the impact of their abusive or toxic actions. They call you "crazy," pathologize your emotions, disavow having said or done something hurtful, or tell you that you're imagining the abuse.

Stonewalling and the silent treatment. This pattern is illustrated by the toxic person who chronically shuts down conversations before they begin or ignores you completely when you try to speak to them. They withdraw abruptly during conflicts and give you the silent treatment even when all is going well in your relationship.

Blatant lack of empathy and penchant for exploitation. Conscienceless acts like infidelity, abandonment during times of need (like when you're sick), and placing you in harm's way are clear signs of the narcissist's deficient compassion and empathy. Sociopaths and psychopaths go one step further by showing little to no remorse for their actions, sometimes even taking sadistic pleasure in hurting you when you're already down. Or, if they do show remorse, it's often with crocodile tears and sob stories to get you to feel sympathy for them, which momentarily restores the relationship so that the abuse cycle can begin again.

Pathological lying. A narcissist will lie to you about both big and small issues, even irrelevant ones. They do this to maintain control. After all, if you don't realize that they are lying, you will make decisions based on what they tell you rather than on reality. They could lead a double life and engage in multiple affairs, exposing you to both emotional and physical harm in terms of your health. A person who is repeatedly deceptive cannot be trusted. As Martha Stout, PhD, notes in her book *The Sociopath Next Door*, "Deceit is the linchpin of conscienceless behavior" (2005, 157). Malignant narcissists tend to be skilled con artists and liars.

Covert and overt put-downs. Narcissists diminish the self-esteem of their victims by belittling, demeaning, and verbally abusing them. They give you backhanded compliments, employ name-calling, insult you directly, or use a consistently condescending and contemptuous tone when speaking to you. They may rage at you or try to provoke you with insidious comments disguised as "jokes," a common tactic used in verbal abuse.

Controlling and isolating behavior. Narcissistic individuals are highly possessive of their victims and view them as objects. They might try to control how you dress, whether you work or not, and with whom you interact, attempting to cut you off from your social network of friends, family members, and coworkers.

Sabotaging. According to researchers Lange, Paulhus, and Crusius (2017), malicious envy is associated with darker narcissistic personalities, often involving behaviors like deception, sabotage, and spreading rumors about the envied person. Narcissists may attempt to sabotage a victim's success, derail their career opportunities, and ruin the victim's reputation with public humiliation and degradation.

Smear campaigns. This behavior equates to slandering you by telling falsehoods about you, recruiting "allies" in support of terrorizing you, and openly denigrating you. In a professional setting, narcissists may even "blacklist" you from opportunities because you threaten their power in some way.

Sexual coercion or violation. Predatory individuals do not respect sexual boundaries. They may try to sexually violate or coerce you into activities you're not comfortable with, ignoring or overstepping your physical boundaries while doing so.

Financial abuse. Taking your earnings, giving you an "allowance," refusing to let you work to create dependency, and maintaining complete economic control of your shared finances—these are all actions a toxic narcissist may routinely engage in.

Stalking and harassment. These are common behaviors for narcissists, especially when their victims have threatened their power and control by leaving them first. They might show up unexpectedly, call, text, or email you through anonymous accounts, leave threatening voice mails, or follow you. They can also engage in cyberstalking or even use tracking devices to keep an eye on your whereabouts.

Physical abuse. Not all narcissists are physically violent, but it's important to remember that a disordered individual can potentially escalate into violence or engage in violent acts such as choking, punching, pushing, smacking, or even attempted murder. You can gauge your level of danger by taking an assessment developed by security expert Gavin de Becker at https://www.mosaicmethod.com. If you have immediate safety concerns, please get yourself somewhere safe and call the National Domestic Violence Hotline at 1-800-799-7233.

JOURNAL REFLECTION: **Manipulation Inventory**
Which of the manipulation tactics listed above, if any, do you experience most frequently in your relationships?

The Psychology of Malignant Toxic People

Narcissists with antisocial traits, paranoia, and sadism are known as "malignant narcissists" (Kernberg 1984). It's important to be aware of what they are capable of doing. On Christmas Eve 2002, a young pregnant mother went missing in Modesto, California. When questioned, her husband, Scott Peterson, refused a polygraph test. He claimed to have been out fishing on his boat during her disappearance. Scott appeared to be a loving husband and was so superficially charming that he had many fooled as he inserted himself into the investigation and lied about his involvement in his wife's murder.

At the vigil for Laci Peterson and her unborn son, Scott called his girlfriend, Amber Frey, and told her an elaborate tale about how he was spending New Year's Eve in Paris. Chillingly enough, Scott had lied to Amber at the onset of their relationship and told her he had lost his wife weeks before Laci was murdered. Unbeknownst to him, Amber was part of a sting operation that ultimately exposed Scott. When Laci and her unborn son's bodies were discovered in San Francisco Bay, Scott was found and arrested. He'd changed the color of his hair and was carrying his brother's ID and $10,000 in cash near the Mexican border.

Most of society cannot fathom what would cause someone to kill their loving spouse, let alone their unborn child—all while living a double life. Though extreme in its tragic ending, Laci Peterson's story is not unlike that of many victims of narcissists and sociopaths: the abuse takes place behind closed doors, in secrecy, and the victims themselves may not even realize the true danger they're in until it's too late. Scott Peterson was perceived as a doting soon-to-be dad and husband, the "nice guy" next door. A superficially charming and glib demeanor is common among these toxic types and hides the true character of a wolf in sheep's clothing. Yet Scott's acute lack of empathy and remorseless ability to discard his family to start a new life with his girlfriend ultimately exposed him for what he is: a malignant predator. To a sociopath, anything that stands in the way of what they desire can be annihilated without remorse.

Such types are not toxic in the benign, frustrating way that garden-variety manipulators are. They are outright dangerous. And although most do not commit murder, they do cause irreparable harm to others in the form of lifelong trauma. What is known as "narcissistic abuse" is an insidious, covert form of violence in which an emotionally abusive narcissist or sociopath chronically gaslights, stonewalls, manipulates, coerces, and controls their victims. Sometimes they perform horrific acts of violence or drive their victims to suicide.

In order to better tackle their manipulation tactics, we have to understand the psychology of narcissistic individuals. The number of narcissistic, sociopathic, and psychopathic personalities in our society cannot be underestimated, with clinical psychologist Martha Stout positing that one in twenty-five Americans is a sociopath (2005, 6). This is a terrifying number to consider, since sociopaths have no conscience, actively exploit others for their personal profit and pleasure, and feel no remorse for their actions. Even if the number of predatory individuals in our society were low, given that these toxic types build harems of admirers, they can affect many victims throughout their lifetime, with highly sensitive and empathic people as their primary targets.

Traits of Personality Disorders

According to some therapists, it is estimated that over 158 million people in the United States are negatively affected by someone else's personality disorder, specifically narcissistic personality disorder and antisocial personality disorder (Bonchay 2017):

Narcissistic personality disorder is associated with an excessive sense of entitlement, a need for admiration, a tendency to exploit others, a callous lack of empathy, a haughty sense of superiority, and feelings of grandiosity.

Antisocial personality disorder (associated with the more colloquial terms "sociopath" and "psychopath") can include these traits along with a lack of remorse or conscience, superficial and glib charm, exploitation for personal profit and pleasure, and a history of criminal acts (APA 2013).

Those who meet the criteria for what's known as the "dark triad" (narcissism, psychopathy, and Machiavellianism) can be quite dangerous and sadistic. They use their cognitive empathy to intellectually assess what hurts their victims the most. They gain pleasure from inflicting pain but lack the affective empathy to care about how their actions impact others.

How could someone be capable of such cruelty and indifference to their own kin? Surely, we assume, this behavior must stem from some sort of psychosis or insanity, but that is not the case for the character-disordered. Malignant toxic types don't have a deficit in sanity; rather, they are lacking in pro-social emotions that might otherwise inhibit their aggression toward others. We've learned about the overly empathic brains of HSPs; now consider that the brains of narcissists and psychopaths are quite the opposite. Narcissists have been shown in studies to have gray matter abnormalities in areas of the brain related to empathy (Schulze et al. 2013). Furthermore, research has shown that psychopaths have structural and functional abnormalities in their orbitofrontal and ventromedial prefrontal cortex, the part of the brain implicated in empathy and guilt, and in the amygdala, which plays a key role in fear and emotion processing (Glenn and Raine 2014). The connectivity between these two regions is also disrupted, preventing emotion-related information from the amygdala signaling threat or harm to others from informing the psychopath's decision-making (Motzkin, et al. 2011).

Unlike individuals who are reactively aggressive due to fear and threat, psychopaths exhibit reduced responses in their amygdala, and they engage in instrumental aggression that is premeditated to achieve a reward or goal. They are not "lashing out" in pain or in response to a perceived threat; rather, they are operating from a lack of empathy, deficient reactions to aversive stimuli, fearlessness, and emotional poverty when abusing others.

Psychopaths also lack a "moral sense." They demonstrate deficits in several other areas of the brain: the hippocampus, which helps in the recall of emotional memories and fear conditioning that would allow them to learn from consequences; the striatum, which is tied to their greater need for reward and stimulation; and regions of the brain known as the "moral neural network," like the posterior cingulate, the medial prefrontal cortex, and angular gyrus, which relate to moral reasoning, perspective-taking and the experience of emotions (Glenn and Raine 2014). These differences in the brain are thought to contribute to a psychopath's heightened sensation-seeking, reward-oriented behavior, and deceitful manipulativeness, while impairing their empathy, moral decision-making, inhibition, and fear of punishment.

Narcissistic personality disorder and antisocial personality disorder (distinct diagnoses from psychopathy, but with many overlapping traits) are very difficult to treat. It is widely agreed upon by therapists and experts that many narcissists on the high level of the spectrum are unlikely to change and are unwilling to seek treatment unless it suits their agendas in some way. They may *appear* to change temporarily to further their self-interest or to manipulate those around them, but permanent change is unlikely, as their behaviors are hardwired patterns that have been present since childhood.

Although there is no clinical verdict on what causes pathological narcissism, victims of narcissists and psychopaths may assume that the malignant individual is acting out from their own trauma and feel compelled to "fix" them. Yet the more callous and fearless the predator is, the less likely this is to be the case. While childhood abuse has been linked to the secondary high-anxious subtype of psychopathy, primary low-anxious psychopaths are less likely to have been abused and do not experience mental health problems like post-traumatic symptoms as frequently (Kimonis et al. 2012; Tatar et al. 2012). In fact, one study showed that some individuals develop narcissistic traits from being overvalued, spoiled, and taught an excessive sense of entitlement (Brummelman et al. 2015). Whereas overvaluing and spoiling a child is also a form of mistreatment, it's not typically the traumatic childhood we assume narcissistic types to have had. Narcissists on the lower end of the spectrum may be shame-based and more vulnerable, but it is usually grandiose and entitled narcissists on the high end of the spectrum who tend to terrorize their victims. We simply don't always know the root of their disorder, and no matter the traumatic upbringing they might have had, their abuse is still a choice. If a narcissist is on the high end of the spectrum, their abuse is often inflicted with perverse pleasure. There are many victims of abuse, including HSPs, who choose *not* to abuse.

These disorders are often associated with manipulative and abusive behavior. Clinical psychologist Ramani Durvasula, an expert on relationship abuse, notes, "I've done research and work in the area of domestic violence or what's also called intimate partner violence; most people who perpetrate domestic violence are either narcissistic or psychopathic. So there is danger there; in other words, they will dispose of you if you get in their way" (2018).

Such was the tragic case for victims like Laci Peterson, but she is not the only one. Chris Watts murdered his pregnant wife, Shanann Watts, her unborn child, and their two small children. He buried his two daughters in oil wells and lied to news reporters about their whereabouts. He even went so far as to claim that his wife had killed the children first, leading him into a homicidal rage. While on the extreme end, this type of "setup" to slander the true victims is all too familiar to those of us who have dealt with narcissists who tried to paint themselves as innocent of their deeds by shifting blame onto their victims.

In another horrific case, army sergeant Emile Cilliers attempted to murder his wife on two different occasions: first, by staging a gas leak in their house, which could have also killed their children, then by tampering with her parachute while skydiving. Thankfully, she survived the 4,000-foot fall. It was discovered that Emile, much like Scott Peterson and Chris Watts, also had a double life. The police uncovered thousands of texts to various extramarital partners. He had numerous affairs and had unprotected sex with prostitutes. He, too, was planning to run off with a girlfriend he had on the side.

There Can Be Danger in Unpredictability

The eerily similar patterns of sociopaths and psychopaths reveal how dangerous they can be and how they become violent in extreme cases. The most dangerous toxic people aren't always those in prison—they are the ones who can pass as very "nice" people, as pillars of their community, all while inflicting great harm behind closed doors. They can turn on the charm and sweep you into a whirlwind romance with their magnetic and disarming charisma.

As therapist Andrea Schneider, who specializes in working with victims of narcissistic abuse, tells me, "Whether an abusive, narcissistic person appears garden variety or malignant, it's important to remember that there is no crystal ball to predict an abusive person's behavior. Many victims are caught up in cognitive dissonance or FOG (fear, obligation, guilt) as a result of the abuse and may not be able to accurately assess the true threat of an abusive individual. That's why, if you feel your life is in any way in danger or you're being chronically abused, always reach out for help. The behaviors you witness are more important to take note of rather than overly focusing on a diagnostic label, because disordered individuals can be very unpredictable."

Why You May Fall Prey to Toxic Individuals

You may be wondering why you would even get entangled with a malignant type in the first place. After all, as an HSP, you have nothing in common with a psychopathic individual. You are highly empathic; they are highly manipulative and destructive. Yet it is your greatest assets that often make you an appealing target for such a predator.

Empathy, conscientiousness, sentimentality, resilience, a giving nature—these are all qualities that malignant toxic people use against their targets to exploit them. In a healthy relationship where both partners are empathetic and emotionally attuned, traits like these help the relationship flourish. In a relationship with a narcissist, however, these traits are exploited and used against you. Since highly sensitive individuals tend to make decisions based on their own sense of right and wrong, they are likely to project *their* own sense of morality and conscience onto the narcissist and assume that the narcissist, too, possesses that same degree of empathy for others.

This assumption is usually dangerously wrong and can lead HSPs to violate their own core values and boundaries just to cater to the narcissist's needs, hoping the narcissist will reciprocate or change their toxic behavior. What we should remember when dealing with narcissistic individuals is that they don't have empathy for our pain or distress; they will choose to put themselves first. They are not above violating the rights of others to meet their own self-interest.

There is a parasitic dynamic between an HSP and a narcissist. The HSP acts as the "host" to the narcissist as they drain us of our resources. During the "love bombing" phase of a relationship, when we're initially showered with attention and affection (more on this in chapter 3), the narcissist infiltrates our life with a combination of charm and manipulation, equipped with a hidden agenda to "feed" on the HSP. The HSP becomes invested in the narcissist, believing they've met their soul mate (or perfect business partner or ideal friend). When the tides turn and the narcissist's false mask slips, the HSP rationalizes the narcissist's abusive behavior—we assume that trauma, insecurities, or fear of intimacy is what's preventing them from establishing a healthy connection. The truth is, what we are witnessing is the narcissist's true character. The narcissist establishes relationships for one purpose only: *narcissistic supply*—any form of praise, attention, admiration, ego-stroking, money, sex, or resources that the relationship grants them.

The heightened empathy of HSPs ultimately places us at risk when we encounter toxic individuals. It causes us to view them from our own moral perspective, seeing them in an overly sympathetic light and dismissing, rationalizing, or minimizing red flags. This is both erroneous and self-destructive. Traci Stein, PhD, points out that, because most people perceive the actions of narcissists through a societally "accepted moral code" that condemns behaviors like lying and harming others, we will exert ourselves to find excuses or justifications for someone's duplicitous behavior rather than confronting their malicious motives (2016). How many of us have rationalized a toxic person's unacceptable behavior by believing that they must just be "suffering" from low self-esteem, a "bad day," or a "troubled" childhood? I bet that if you are reading this book, this sounds familiar.

The Three Steps a Manipulator Takes to Get Your Pity

When you are highly empathic, you try to see the best in others and "help" those you think are hurting, especially if they use a *pity ploy* on you—any action that invites sympathy for the purpose of manipulation—to get you to see them as the victims when they are really the perpetrators. Toxic people and narcissists may wax on about their bad childhood, their addiction problems, and their hardships to get you to feel sorry for them. According to Martha Stout, these perverse appeals to sympathy after violence or aggression are the hallmarks of "unscrupulous people" (2005, 107). Due to a manipulator's professed pain, you readily make excuses for their so-called mistakes. This allows the abuse cycle to continue, uninterrupted. It is therefore essential to break down how a pity ploy works so you can recognize when one is being pulled on you.

Step 1: The toxic person acts remorseful with crocodile tears or fake apologies. But they never actually change behaviors in the long term.

Step 2: They rationalize or justify their abuse. They might describe their suffering or claim their mistreatment of you was a misunderstanding, unintentional, or out of their control (for example, blaming it on alcohol or something you did). The abuse cycle starts again once you forgive and reconcile with them.

Step 3: If the pity ploy fails to elicit the desired reaction, the manipulator labels the victim bitter, judgmental, selfish, or otherwise unhinged. They lash out in rage, use gaslighting, and continue their manipulation until the victim is beaten into submission.

You might continuously walk through these steps, over and over again, because a conscientious person like yourself is concerned about the welfare of others and has a track record of following through on obligations to others. Narcissists know you have this inherent sense of responsibility, and they trust that highly conscientious people will undertake those perceived responsibilities, even if it places them in harm's way.

While narcissists feel little remorse for harmful transgressions, victims feel morally apprehensive about exposing *them*, about retaliating, betraying the relationship in any way, or stepping back from their perceived obligations. Once again, your positive trait of integrity, which benefits you in relationships with empathetic individuals, becomes ammunition in toxic relationships.

Malignant toxic types know that conscientious people will give them the benefit of the doubt, walk on eggshells to avoid conflict (which can be highly demanding on the HSP's nervous system), fall prey to pity ploys, and care deeply for others despite any harm they pose. Clinical psychologist George Simon, an expert on the character-disordered, puts it this way: "Disturbed characters most often target folks possessing two qualities they don't possess: conscientiousness and excessive agreeableness (i.e., deference). So, it's a solid conscience that makes you most vulnerable to narcissistic manipulation. Manipulators use guilt and shame as their prime weapons. But you have to have the capacity for shame and guilt for the tactics to work. Disturbed characters lack that capacity. Conscientious folks have it in spades" (2018).

Due to the depression and anxiety that can arise from conflict with narcissistic individuals, you as an HSP are very vulnerable to the psychological and physical effects of narcissistic manipulation, especially if you're unaware of the manipulation and rationalize toxic behaviors. Even after you become aware, it can be difficult to leave an abuser when you've been severely traumatized.

JOURNAL REFLECTION: **Pity Ploy Defense**

Think about a time when you rationalized a manipulator's mistreatment of you. Did you feel sorry for them and let them off easy, instead of holding them accountable and presenting them with tangible consequences? What will you do differently next time?

Why We Stay: A Biochemical Addiction

"Why is it so difficult for me to just leave and cease contact?" This is one of the most common questions I get from highly sensitive, empathic people dealing with toxic relationships. Answering this question is vital, because it is not the merits of the person or the relationship that keep us there. No, it's something far more dangerous and addictive.

Trauma from toxic relationships hijacks our "emotional brain," affecting areas like the amygdala and hippocampus, while bringing the thinking part of our brain, the prefrontal cortex, offline. These areas of the brain affect our emotions, self-control and impulsivity, reactions to threat, memory, learning, planning, and decision making (van der Kolk 2014). Trauma also interferes with the communication between the right and left hemispheres of the brain, deactivating the left hemisphere, which causes us to lose *executive functioning*—the ability to organize our experiences into a coherent narrative, solve problems, and make beneficial decisions.

Remember this before you blame yourself for behaving in what appeared to be a nonsensical manner; your brain was working against you in a time of extreme chaos. At the root of abusive relationships is what trauma experts label *trauma bonding*—creating ties during intense emotional experiences in which we bond with our "captors" to survive.

Patrick Carnes, PhD, refers to this as a *betrayal bond*. "Exploitive relationships create betrayal bonds. These occur when a victim bonds with someone who is destructive to him or her. Thus the hostage becomes the champion of the hostage taker, the incest victim covers for the parent, and the exploited employee fails to expose the wrongdoing of the boss.... [This] is a mind-numbing, highly addictive attachment to the people who have hurt you" (2015, 6). Carnes describes how victims in such a bond try to "convert" abusers into nonabusers by trying to help them "understand" that what they're doing is wrong. Victims often turn to self-blame for not being able to succeed in this task, and these trauma bonds cause them to lose trust in their own sense of reality, placing them at greater risk of danger. Abuse victims try to prevent more abuse from happening by attempting to make the relationship work, but inevitably, this only results in more pain.

Understanding why we stay can help us shift away from self-blame and exit relationships that harm us. Similar to the phenomenon of Stockholm syndrome, trauma bonding causes you, the survivor held captive by the abuser, to defend the abuser even after enduring horrific acts of emotional or physical violence. This is a bond that is difficult to break, and predatory types do everything in their power to sustain this bond with their victims to further terrorize them. It doesn't help that in any toxic relationship, our own brains work against us. The trauma bond is exacerbated by biochemical bonding with our abusers; hormones and chemicals like oxytocin, dopamine, serotonin, cortisol, and adrenaline all play a key role in causing us to feel addicted to toxic people.

A Dopamine High Like No Other

Love is stimulating to the pleasure and reward centers of our brain, so imagine its effect on the brain of an HSP! For example, rats that have had their pleasure centers electrically stimulated will do pretty much *anything* to reexperience the cerebral voltage, even risk getting shocked, to press the lever that will stimulate them *thousands* of times—not unlike the many times we seek to relive the pleasure of the "honeymoon phase" with a narcissist, despite the excruciating pain we experience with them (Olds and Milner 1954).

We assume that we should "know" better, right? But the problem isn't just knowing better—it's also about how we *feel*. Toxic love, surprisingly enough, creates a dopamine high like no other, and HSPs can experience such emotions on a heightened level. Dopamine is the neurotransmitter associated with the pleasure center of the brain, and it plays a powerful role in desire and addiction. Narcissistic individuals love bomb us early on in the relationship with excessive praise and attention. When we are flooded with dopamine from this showering of love, we experience intense feelings of euphoria that are not unlike a drug addiction. In fact, researchers Andreas Bartels and Semir Zeki (2000) discovered that the brains of people in love resemble the brains of cocaine addicts. Helen Fisher (2016) also confirmed that love activates several of the same regions of the brain associated with addiction and craving, even when one is rejected. This is why you may experience a deep withdrawal effect from your narcissistic partner when they begin to pull away from you and engage in what's known as *hot-and-cold behavior*: drawing you close only to push you away.

Our brains can be rewired to fixate on those who are bad for us. According to Susan Carnell, PhD, abusive tactics like hot-and-cold behavior work well with our dopamine system because studies show that dopamine flows more readily when the rewards are given out on an unpredictable schedule (2012). When there are intermittent periods of pleasure mixed in with pain, it alerts the brain to "pay attention" as a form of survival and to work harder to get the reward, which may not be a sure thing. On the other hand, when we overindulge in the pleasurable experience, there tends to be less dopamine released because our brains realize we don't have to work for it to obtain it again.

Rewarding Experiences → Release of
Dopamine → Causes Us to Want It Again

Overindulging in the Rewarding
Experience → Less Dopamine Released

Intermittent Rewards → Dopamine Flows More Readily

The salience theory of dopamine suggests that negative experiences, too, release dopamine, causing us to become highly attuned to things that are important to our survival (Wang and Tsein 2011; Fowler et al. 2007). It's no surprise that Fisher (2016) discovered that this "frustration-attraction" experience that we encounter in adverse relationships actually *heightens* these feelings of romantic love rather than diminishes them.

The very nature of hot-and-cold behavior in a toxic relationship with a narcissist actually serves our unhealthy addiction to them. Pleasure and pain combined make for a more "rewarding" experience for our brains than pleasure alone, and our brains pay more attention to these relationships as a result. A relationship with a narcissist, which is wrought with constant conflict, gaslighting and confusion, a persistent sense of uncertainty, tumultuous arguments, or even abuse, makes us work harder for the perceived rewards of the relationship. It creates reward circuits in our brains that can be even stronger than those in healthier relationships.

JOURNAL REFLECTION: **Dopamine Rush**

Think about the most stable relationships or friendships you've had. How did they feel? Did they feel secure, boring, joyful? In contrast, reflect on the toxic relationships you've had that have included hot-and-cold behavior. Did they have an addictive or exciting quality to them, even if they weren't healthy?

Oxytocin's Role in Blind Trust

Oxytocin is famously known as the "cuddle" or "love hormone," released during touching, sexual intercourse, and orgasm, promoting attachment and trust (Watson 2013). This same hormone creates a bond between mother and child at birth. During the love bombing phases of our relationship with a narcissist, the effects of this hormone can be quite strong, especially as we become physically intimate with our partner.

Our brains have a tendency to blindly trust those we love—even those who've betrayed us. Research shows that the release of oxytocin can lead to increased trust and continued investment in another person, even after breaches of trust have occurred (Baumgartner et al. 2008). So when we encounter infidelity and pathological lying from narcissistic partners, our physical bond to them can still overpower us to the point of continuing to invest in them, despite evidence of their transgressions. Oxytocin causes us to trust this toxic person, even if they are not trustworthy.

That's why slowing down physical intimacy in the early stages of dating can be helpful to better assess and discern whether the person you are investing in is worth it. Without the fog of sexual intimacy clouding our perceptions, we can better manage our emotions and temper them with rationality.

JOURNAL REFLECTION: The Oxytocin Fog

In the toxic relationships you've had, was there a "fast-forwarding" of physical intimacy? Did that in any way blind you to the person's true attributes?

The Infatuation of Serotonin, Cortisol, and Adrenaline

Psychiatrist Donatella Marazziti discovered that people in love have around the same levels of serotonin as those with obsessive-compulsive disorder (OCD) (Marazziti et al. 1999). Serotonin is known for its role in regulating mood (especially anxiety and depression). People with OCD, along with HSPs, tend to have unusually low levels of this neurotransmitter. This low level of serotonin can cause obsessive thoughts. Knowing this, our uncontrollable thoughts about a narcissistic individual make a whole lot more sense.

Not only do serotonin levels decrease when we fall in love, but also levels of the stress hormone cortisol rise to help us with the fight-or-flight response, which prepares us for "battle" against a perceived emergency with a heightened sense of alertness (van der Kolk 2014). High levels of cortisol also strengthen the impact of our fearful memories and can cause trauma to become "trapped" within our bodies, leading to physical overwhelm and numerous health problems (Drexler et al. 2015).

This combination of serotonin levels lowering and cortisol levels rising creates an intense preoccupation and infatuation with our partner or love interest—our relationship with them feels like a matter of life or death. This explains why we have an obsessive tendency to constantly think about the ones we love, even if they are detrimental to our well-being.

Serotonin Levels Fall + Cortisol Levels Rise → Intense Preoccupation with Partner

Adrenaline and norepinephrine also prepare the body for the fight-or-flight response, and these also play a role in this biochemical addiction (Klein 2013). When we see the person we love, adrenaline is released, causing our hearts to race and our palms to sweat. This same hormone is tied to fear—something we have a lot of when we're dealing with a narcissist.

Adrenaline + Fear + Arousal → Attraction

Ask any dating coach and they'll tell you that dates paired with excitement and fear are likely to be more memorable, creating an intense bond to the person in our brains. Research confirms that arousal from fear and attraction are linked, so when we share an intense, scary experience with our partner (such as riding a roller coaster together), we can become more attached and drawn to them as a result (Dutton and Aron 1974). It's no wonder that our fearful experiences with a narcissistic individual trick our brains into believing we have an inseparable bond.

JOURNAL REFLECTION: Adrenaline Junkie

What kinds of fearful or dangerous experiences did you have in the toxic relationships in your life? Was there usually a period of peace and comfort after these events?

Perhaps you're wondering, *Well, okay, I know now how these bonds come to be—but what do I do about them?* Not to worry! In chapter 5, you'll learn specifically how to tackle these biochemical bonds and how to replace them with healthier outlets, ultimately allowing you to break the addiction to a narcissist.

EXERCISE: Trauma Bond Checklist

Here's another checklist you can use to help you determine whether you're in a trauma bond with a toxic manipulator. Go through the following statements, checking all that apply.

☐ You feel physically and emotionally exhausted after even just one interaction with this person. Your energy feels drained, and you may even feel immobilized or paralyzed.

☐ You experience physical symptoms of anxiety around this person— for example, your heart beats faster, your palms sweat, you develop sudden migraines, your skin breaks out, or you experience gastrointestinal or other health issues that seem to come out of nowhere.

☐ Your productivity suffers. You experience interruptions in learning, memory, planning, focusing, judgment, and decision making when around or after interacting with this person.

☐ You find yourself being taken advantage of repeatedly—rather than being in a reciprocal relationship, you tend to be the "giver." The other person "uses" you for your resources, your time, and your efforts, usually without returning the favor.

☐ You experience diminished self-esteem after being around this person. Their comments and toxic behaviors make you feel worthless, lacking, or ashamed of yourself in some way.

☐ You are aware that they are manipulative and toxic, but you feel unable to "let go" of the relationship. Due to your trauma bond with them, you find yourself rationalizing, minimizing, or denying their abusive behavior. You feel an intense addiction to them, regardless of how terribly they treat you.

☐ Even when you're no longer in their presence, you find yourself obsessing over their words and actions, unable to make sense of who they really are. You develop an intense preoccupation with the relationship. A conversation with them over something that *should* have a simple solution leaves you feeling disoriented and confused.

☐ Your emotions have a "yo-yo" effect whenever you're communicating with them. One second, you're confident and self-assured. The next, you're feeling deflated and traumatized. This is due to the manipulator's "Jekyll and Hyde" behavior—they're sweet when they need something and mean when they want to establish control.

☐ Your energy and mood lift after you are away from this toxic person for a few days or weeks, however long it takes you to "detox" from them.

☐ You find yourself second-guessing everything, including your perception of reality. The toxic manipulator often denies things they said or did, and you start to wonder if you're "imagining" things. They gaslight you into believing that your experiences and emotions aren't valid.

☐ You experience a high degree of conflicting thoughts, beliefs, and emotions whenever you're interacting with this person (in psychology, we call this *cognitive dissonance*, which can be an extremely disorienting and distressing state). They can switch from kind to spiteful quickly, and this leaves you feeling increasingly anxious and confused about their true character and intentions.

☐ You experience a deflated sense of self-esteem and agency over your life. You develop feelings of powerlessness and learned helplessness whenever you're in active communication with this person.

If you've realized you're an HSP with a habit of becoming entangled with toxic people, know that you're not alone. Although some of the traits that make you an HSP can leave you vulnerable to emotional predators, you also have traits that can be used as strengths to detect toxic people, establish solid boundaries, and tackle their manipulation head-on.

As a reminder of the relationship red flags summarized in this chapter, refer to the "Healthy Versus Toxic Relationships" chart provided at http://www.newharbinger.com/45304, where you'll find additional supplementary materials to complement this book. You can print out and post this chart somewhere you'll see it every day to keep you focused on what to look for—and what to stay away from—in future relationships.

CHAPTER TWO

Benign and Malignant
The Five Types of Toxic People

One of my former friends was obsessed with having a boyfriend; she would jump from relationship to relationship, spending most of her time, energy, and savings on each new beau. I would often offer support and validation through her relationship problems. However, when I suffered a grueling loss, she abandoned me in the days that followed and accused me of being "selfish" for expecting her support and for letting her know I was hurt by her behavior.

My former friend may not have been a malignant narcissist, but she was still a toxic person, which is why I ended up cutting ties with her altogether, even when she continued to reach out to me to try to repair the friendship. Her self-centeredness and inability to care about anything other than her romantic relationships, coupled with her abandonment during one of the toughest periods of my life, convinced me this was not a friendship worth saving.

This is an example of a "benign" toxic type personality, whereas narcissistic and sociopathic/psychopathic personalities fall into the "malignant" toxic type category. The spectrum of toxicity requires that we take into account the context of the person's behaviors, the frequency with which they use manipulation to get their way, how receptive they are to feedback, and whether they address your concerns empathically and effectively. You must adapt boundaries based on your own levels of personal safety and perceived harm.

There are five common types of toxic people—three fall under the benign umbrella and two under malignant. I have included stories that illustrate just how they operate and offer tips for how to address the problems their behaviors cause you.

Benign Toxicity

Not all toxic people are malignant narcissists, nor do they take pleasure in causing harm. Some suffer from a different disorder or histrionic tendencies; others struggle with family-of-origin issues, self-centeredness, selfishness, or past traumas. They may still engage in gaslighting and projection, like my friend did when confronted; however, it is not their *primary* way of connecting to others. Their patterns of behavior may not always warrant cutting off all contact or assigning them a rigid label, but setting boundaries with them is crucial nonetheless. Toxicity is still toxicity, and it must be addressed one way or the other.

Toxic Personality Type #1: Garden-Variety Boundary-Steppers

These types of toxic people are the most benign out of the bunch, but they can still be harmful and are unaware of how toxic they are. They habitually cross over your boundaries by talking over you, invading your personal space, asking more of you than you can give, bestowing unsolicited advice, wasting your time, being flaky, or breaking commitments. They may be loud and self-absorbed, selfish, or otherwise unable to read social cues.

Nancy was the nosiest colleague at work. She would walk around each and every cubicle in the morning and talk her coworkers' ears off. Then she would start in on the unsolicited advice. "We just got a new Labrador puppy—oh, he's just the cutest, I could die.... Taylor, you know, you'd look prettier with some blue earrings. You know what you need? How about I set you up on a blind date? I know this handsome man, Tom, from my old accounting firm. You need to get out there!"

Steve's overbearing mother, Clara, would constantly call him every day, even at work, to "check up" on him. She had made this a habit after he got into a car accident. She was sincerely worried about him, but she expressed that worry in unhealthy ways.

How you might set boundaries with someone like Nancy or Clara: Politely explain your unavailability and use your emotional reserves to cut these interactions short rather than engaging and adding fuel to the fire. Your energy can easily become drained by a boundary-trespasser, even if they don't mean any ill will. Before Nancy launches into a full-on discussion about pets and blind dates, you might interrupt her with something like, "Hey, Nancy, I'm actually really busy right now. And I'm not looking to date anyone at the moment." If she insists on continuing, you can excuse yourself.

Get into the habit of making conversations with boundary-breakers shorter and shorter each time. If you were Steve, you could let Clara know that you won't be available to take her phone calls during the week, but that you will check in via text occasionally, offering one day a week for a regular call. Follow through by refusing her personal phone calls at work. Gently "ease" boundary-steppers into your unavailability, and it will become more of an ingrained habit for them to respect your limits because they have no other choice. They'll usually move on to a more receptive target.

Toxic Personality Type #2: Crazy-Makers and Attention-Seekers

A step above the garden-variety toxic person are the "crazy-makers" and "attention-seekers." These types have one selfish agenda: to have the focus be on them at all times, even if the feedback they receive is negative. They will create drama, introduce conflict, or showboat to garner praise out of an overwhelming need for attention. While they can be incredibly draining, frustrating, and demanding of your attention, they are a bit easier to work with than your more malignant types.

Heidi loved to be the center of attention. She would wear provocative clothing every day at work, flirt with her male colleagues, and loudly discuss details from her personal life at the office. Heidi's pathological need for attention was so all-encompassing that her coworkers found it hard to focus on their work when she was always coming around and attempting to monopolize every conversation. When she didn't get the attention she needed, Heidi would become upset and lash out at feeling neglected.

One of her coworkers, Laura, felt especially triggered by Heidi because she was constantly overshadowed by her in meetings. This was because Heidi would interrupt her while she was discussing her ideas. Heidi would also come by Laura's desk every morning and just dive into tales of her latest romantic adventures, distracting Laura at the beginning of the day.

How to set boundaries with someone like Heidi: Withdraw your attention. Attention-seekers crave your emotional reactions and energy; if they don't get what they need from you, they'll move on to a more sustainable form of fuel. In this specific example, Laura might set boundaries with Heidi by taking her aside and letting her know that she'd appreciate it if Heidi would stop interrupting her at meetings. She might say, "While I value your input, I'd like to get my own ideas into the next staff meeting without being interrupted. Also, I'd prefer if, in the mornings, we could limit our chats—I am very busy in the mornings, and I don't have the time or energy to speak with people."

If Heidi refuses to abide by these boundaries, Laura might then decide to have a chat with their manager about these issues or disrupt Heidi's pattern by saying, "Excuse me, let me just finish what I was saying first," politely but firmly each time she interrupts. The tangible consequence of being called out publicly can embarrass an attention-seeker into getting the spotlight elsewhere; disrupting their ploys can also help make you a less savory target for someone who is looking for an ego stroke. When you refocus the attention back on you and your original intention, the attention-seeker is left with fewer options to continue their crazy-making with you.

Toxic Personality Type #3: Emotional Vampires

"Emotional vampire" is usually used as a catchall term in other books and articles to encompass many toxic types. In this book, the term will specifically refer to toxic people who are capable of empathy but profusely drain your energy with their demands.

Lorena's mother was an emotional vampire. Seldom would she check in with her daughter unless she wanted something. Her mother was so emotionally needy, she would take up Lorena's time and attention whenever she was in crisis, but she'd dismiss Lorena when her daughter needed her. She would show up at Lorena's house unannounced, demand to see her grandchildren, and bombard her with endless stories of being victimized. Lorena struggled to set boundaries with her mother. She felt guilty about not acquiescing to her mother's orders, even as an adult, especially when her mother tried to guilt-trip her. Yet she knew that whenever *she* desired help, her mother was nowhere to be found.

How to set boundaries with someone like Lorena's mother: Have a straightforward, firm discussion laying out your boundaries. A great general phrase to repeat with toxic people is, "I would love to help you, but I just don't have the emotional bandwidth for this." Set tangible boundaries and specific consequences for trespassing those boundaries. Implement these consequences each and every time they are trespassed. Lorena might have a discussion with her mother in which she tells her, "I can't be available every time you need me. I am afraid I won't be able to allow you to visit unless you tell me in advance when you're coming." And after this discussion, Lorena would follow through on this by keeping her phone off, refusing to answer calls unless in an emergency, and cutting the visit short should her mother decide to show up unannounced.

It is the *implementation of boundaries*, rather than just words alone, that is so important when dealing with energy vampires. You have to "cut off" their supply if you want your energy to be reserved for more important things, regardless of how the vampires try to guilt-trip or shame you. It's crucial to "starve" an energy vampire by cutting off parasitic and one-sided interactions. If you're no longer playing your role as host, they will inevitably move on to someone who will.

CLEAR UP for Benign Toxicity

To more effectively communicate limits with garden-variety toxic people, use the CLEAR UP acronym I've devised. HSPs who have problems with setting boundaries tend to struggle with anticipated conflict, with saying "no," and with negotiating with benign toxic people. The CLEAR UP tool can help you master conflict and assert yourself in a healthy way.

Context

Lay down the law

Exercise boundaries

Appreciation

Repetition

Unity

Power posing

NOTE: This acronym is meant to be used only with nonabusive individuals. For it to work, people must be willing to listen to your boundaries. Those who are narcissistic may become enraged when you set a boundary, regardless of how constructively you express it. Your safety comes first and foremost, so use these steps only with people who have proven to be receptive to your communication. Later in this chapter, we will talk more about how CLEAR UP can be adapted to communicate with malignant narcissists, as those types demand different strategies than more garden-variety toxic people. If you fear you are in any kind of danger, avoid face-to-face confrontation altogether.

Context. This involves describing the situation clearly to provide context—it's the conversation starter that ignites a larger dialogue about the problem and its potential solutions. Take Natalie, for example, who wants to set boundaries with her boyfriend about calling her late at night. She can lay out the situation clearly by saying something like, "When you call me in the middle of the night, it wakes me up and I have trouble falling asleep again."

Lay down the law. Describe the negative impact of the situation to reinforce *why* this behavior is problematic. In Natalie's case, she might follow up her initial statement with, "When I don't get the proper amount of sleep, it leaves me feeling irritated and groggy throughout the day. I love texting and calling you when we're not together, but not when I'm trying to get a good night's sleep. Doing this places a strain on our relationship."

Exercise boundaries. Set some sort of finite boundary or just say no entirely. Here, Natalie could say, "After my bedtime, please only call or text me in case of emergency. Otherwise, wait until the next day."

Appreciation. Provide positive reinforcement when the person honors your boundaries. This could be anything from a simple "thank you" to a letter of encouragement and appreciation. Natalie might send a good-night text to her boyfriend saying, "Thanks so much for understanding. I am headed off to sleep now, but I just want to say how grateful I am to have a boyfriend who respects my needs."

Repetition. Remain strong in your beliefs, stay focused on your objective (having your rights respected), and refuse to be diverted by the toxic person. You might try the "broken-record technique" of continually stating your points over and over, then walking away from the conversation if the person on the receiving end is unwilling to see your perspective or threatens you.

Unity. Agree to disagree when there are differences of perspective that cannot be overcome. Suggest alternatives if the other person isn't willing to meet your request, or simply ask, "I see we've reached a disagreement. How else can we solve this problem?" Then engage in a constructive dialogue (but only if you determine that the other person is willing to do so in a nonabusive, nonthreatening way; see chapter 3 for tips on how to deal with an abusive person).

Power posing. Even if you are nervous to set a boundary, act confident instead. Actions like maintaining eye contact and using an assertive tone of voice can be useful when navigating conflict with a benign toxic type.

JOURNAL REFLECTION: **Practicing CLEAR UP**

I've provided examples of how to implement the CLEAR UP tool in various situations. But what about in a situation specific to you? Go through each step of the acronym, writing down your thoughts on the following prompts:

- **Context:** Clearly describe an issue you'd like to resolve with a benign toxic person in your life.

- **Lay down the law:** Why is the issue so problematic? What consequences does it have?

- **Exercise boundaries:** Write down one or two ways you can assert a boundary in this situation.

- **Appreciation:** What is one positive way you can reinforce the desired behavior when it's displayed?

- **Repetition:** Come up with a statement you're comfortable with that you can say over and over to get your point across to the toxic individual if they try to divert you or distract you from your goal.

- **Unity:** Think about possible compromises you could make if this person isn't willing to fulfill your request or what you can do to take care of your own needs if they will not or cannot (for example, in Natalie's case, she can preemptively turn off her phone if her boyfriend refuses to stop calling too late).

- **Power posing:** If you're nervous about putting CLEAR UP in practice in your particular situation, what things can you do prior to the meeting or conversation to make you feel energized and confident (like going for a run, repeating positive affirmations, role-playing the conversation with someone else)?

Malignant Toxicity

Now that we've identified the more benign types of toxic people, how about the more malignant types—how do we spot them and how do we deal with them? Although it can be very difficult to communicate with this type of individual, it *is* possible to set boundaries provided that you prioritize your own self-care. To protect ourselves in their presence, we first have to understand the way they think and manipulate. This will give us insight into their agendas, their exploitative ways of approaching the world, and the essential tools needed to safely exit interactions, friendships, and relationships with them.

Toxic Personality Type #4: Narcissists

Narcissists can be dangerously toxic because they lack the empathy to actually care about anybody else's needs but their own. As we discussed in chapter 1, they are self-absorbed, self-centered, and extremely entitled. Depending on the severity of their narcissism, they can also be abusive when any perceived slight induces their narcissistic rage. Here is an acronym to help you remember the characteristics and behaviors of a narcissist:

Never admits to being wrong

Avoids emotions and accountability

Rages if anyone challenges them

Childish when they don't get their way

Instills doubt in their victims

Stonewalls during conflicts

Smears and slanders you

In denial and gaslights you

Subjects you to the silent treatment

Triangulates you and tears you down

Joanne's boyfriend was a narcissist. He would constantly put her down, stonewall her during discussions, and rage at her whenever he thought she was insulting him in some way. He would try to control her and isolate her from her friends and family. He would later gaslight her into believing that the abuse was her fault. He wasn't *always* like this, of course. In the beginning of the relationship, he had been charming and generous. As soon as they entered a long-term relationship, however, he "switched" and revealed his true character. He was cold and unfeeling, rarely caring when she was sick and choosing her most vulnerable moments to launch verbal and emotional attacks.

Setting Boundaries with a Narcissist

An abusive narcissist is not one you can set boundaries with like you can with other everyday toxic people. Your boundaries will be trampled upon and violated without care; so will your rights. When you assert your boundaries, the narcissist will take that information as a clue as to what will most hurt you, and they will use that as ammunition against you to further provoke you. In other words, when you tell a narcissist what hurts you, they will simply do more of that. That's why direct or diplomatic communication with them often falls short of inspiring effective results.

It's important to realize that you have a right to step away from any abusive person, whether the abuse is verbal, emotional, psychological, physical, or sexual. Making a safety plan to get away from an abuser is crucial, especially if there is any threat of violence or physical aggression. In a scenario like this, you would be better off not telling the abuser you are leaving until you have already left and found a safe place. Even then, communication with them should be short, factual, and presented with no door left open for the narcissist to sneak back into your life.

But what if you can't leave a narcissist right away or you have to deal with them in a context you can't avoid, such as the workplace? What if they're a family member you're "stuck" with for life? Here are some tips on how to implement your boundaries with narcissists.

Be emotionally unresponsive to their tactics and provocations. If a toddler was attacking you with insults and tantrums, would you react as if their rantings had any meaning? Don't get me wrong: narcissists are adults and are fully responsible for their behavior. However, you don't have to satisfy their need for attention or a reaction. Whenever possible, observe their rages with the gaze of a detached outsider rather than someone personally involved with them. See how ridiculous their antics are and keep your responses as short and emotionally distant as you possibly can.

Additionally, set a boundary for *yourself* that you will not give in to emotionally manipulative behaviors out of a misplaced sense of obligation or guilt. You didn't cause the narcissist's dysfunction and you're not responsible for remedying it. Unless you are their therapist (and even then, you're there to offer help with boundaries included), it's not your job to "fix" or "cure" someone of their destructive behavior toward others or to tolerate it to your own detriment. It is *their* responsibility to heal and fix themselves. Your duty is to yourself—to discern when someone is toxic to your well-being and to know when to detach and walk away. Do not feed into their crazy-making by reacting the way they want you to.

Keep interactions as short as possible; you can be cordial, but do not engage. Narcissists are master provocateurs who will subject you to dizzying diversion tactics to make you feel off-center and off-balance. That's why you must understand when you are being manipulated and stay focused on your real goals. If your goal is to do your best work at your job, then you must do everything in your power to stay focused on that goal and channel your energy into producing high-quality work rather than feeding into your narcissistic coworker's inevitable mind games. If your goal is to keep custody of your children, do not fall into the trap of sending the narcissist anything that could be used against you in court, no matter how much they try to provoke you (especially in ways that can be documented, like voice mail or text). If your goal is to attend a family event without being harassed by your toxic parent, zero in on spending time with nontoxic family members, politely shutting down conversations that could escalate, and limiting interactions with your narcissistic parent.

Switch the topic when discussions enter unsafe territory. In unavoidable conversations with narcissists, get into the habit of switching the topic or exiting the conversation whenever you can feel things shifting into territory you deem unsafe. If, for example, your narcissistic sister has a habit of bringing up your relationship status as a way to demean you, redirect the conversation to something *she* would be interested in—anything that allows narcissists to talk about themselves will usually distract them from focusing on you.

Brainstorm ways to exit in the future. Just because you feel stuck in a toxic workplace now doesn't mean you'll be there forever. Just because you feel unable to leave a toxic relationship at the moment doesn't mean you have to stay in it for life. Make a plan for the future. Save money, build good credit, and explore your options. If you're married to a narcissist, obtain the services of a divorce financial planner and a lawyer who is well versed in high-conflict personalities. Get support from counselors, support groups, friends, and family members who "get it." Don't let the narcissist in on your plans; they will often try to sabotage them.

Document everything. Documentation with a narcissist is often necessary, especially in the workplace. Keep a record of emails, texts, voice mails, and even audio or video recordings of conversations if your state laws allow it should you ever need proof of exploitation or abuse. Documentation is especially pertinent if you decide to bring a legal case against your abuser, and it can help immensely to resist the gaslighting attempts of a narcissist.

Practice mindfulness and extreme self-care. As we'll discuss in chapter 7, self-care is extremely important in the aftermath of being terrorized by a toxic individual, but it can also be absolutely necessary when your energy is being drained by such people. Healing modalities like meditation, yoga, and visualization of a safe place can all be great tools to ground yourself back in the present moment so that you can bring renewed energy and confidence to any situations you encounter with a narcissist.

Toxic Personality Type #5: Sociopaths and Psychopaths

"Sociopath" and "psychopath" are the more common terms used for people with antisocial personality disorder (ASPD), which is the closest diagnosis we have in the most current version of the Diagnostic and Statistical Manual of Mental Disorders (DSM-5) to describing psychopathy. Someone with ASPD will usually exhibit traits and behaviors such as a pattern of violating the rights of others, a failure to conform to social norms, irritability and aggressiveness, deceitfulness, impulsivity, reckless disregard for self and others, consistent irresponsibility, and lack of remorse. Although not everyone with ASPD is necessarily a sociopath or psychopath, many sociopaths and psychopaths do meet the criteria for ASPD. It's theorized that while sociopaths—more commonly associated with the secondary high-anxious and impulsively hostile subtype described earlier—are produced by their environment, primary low-anxious psychopaths who engage in premeditated, instrumental aggression are born rather than "made." Yet whether you're dealing with a sociopath or a psychopath, they have many overlapping characteristics.

Because antisocial personality disorder cannot be diagnosed in anyone younger than eighteen, those with burgeoning symptoms are usually diagnosed with conduct disorder instead before the age of fifteen. This means they have had a childhood history of troubling behaviors like killing or torturing small animals, bullying others, committing theft, fire-starting, and pathological lying.

To add to our understanding, psychopathy expert Robert Hare, PhD, lists these additional characteristics specific to psychopaths in the Hare Psychopathy Checklist-Revised (PCL-R):

- Glibness and superficial charm
- Pathological lying
- Parasitic lifestyle
- Cunning and manipulative
- Impulsivity
- Callousness and lack of empathy
- Shallow emotions
- Need for stimulation
- Shallow affect
- Irresponsibility

- Failure to take responsibility for their behavior

- Lack of realistic long-term goals

- Sexual promiscuity

- Prone to boredom

- Early behavioral problems or juvenile delinquency

- A number of short-term marital relationships

- Criminal versatility

- Grandiose sense of self

Sociopaths and psychopaths are the most malignant of the toxic types. Not only do they lack empathy, but they also lack remorse and a conscience. Some show violent tendencies and engage in criminal behavior (like the murdering husbands Scott Peterson and Chris Watts you read about earlier), and others are seemingly upstanding citizens who don a mask and commit relational transgressions behind closed doors. Either way, they are likely to engage in high-risk activities, multiple affairs, fraud, duplicitous con artistry, and exploitation of people for their own gain. They leave a trail of victims, and they also take sadistic pleasure in harming others. I've created an acronym below to help you remember the defining traits of a psychopath:

Pathological liar

Superficially charming

Yearns for constant stimulation

Conscienceless and callous con artist

Hides double life

Overestimates self, grandiose

Parasitic lifestyle and promiscuity

Aggressive and impulsive

Taunts and traumatizes for fun

Hides in plain sight

In the infamous case of Mary Jo Buttafuoco, her sociopathic husband, Joey, was able to hide his chronic deception and affair with a young girl even after his mistress decided to physically show up on Mary Jo's doorstep and shoot her in the head. Thankfully, she survived. As she writes in her book *Getting It Through My Thick Skull*, her husband's denials of his infidelity were extremely convincing and so were his excuses. She notes, "One of the most prominent and telling traits of many sociopaths is their fantastic ability to manipulate others and lie for profit, to avoid punishment, or seemingly just for fun … all I can say is that if you haven't ever been under a sociopath's spell, be grateful. They can charm the birds out of the trees and tell you black is white, and have you believing it" (2009, 27).

Setting Boundaries with a Sociopath or Psychopath

Because of the dangers involved, setting boundaries with these predatory types calls for a different set of standards and safety protocols. If you suspect you are dealing with someone who is a sociopath or psychopath, do not pass go. Avoid any face-to-face meetings. You *must* put your safety first. Here are some basic guidelines to follow.

Notify all those you trust that you may be dealing with someone who is potentially dangerous. Tell a trusted therapist, a close friend, or a family member (preferably someone who isn't close to this person) your concerns about what this person might do. This way, at least a few people will know what's going on in case anything should happen to you.

Contact law enforcement if there is any stalking, harassment, or threats involved. The documentation you've collected (texts, email, voice messages, etc.) will corroborate your claims. Do not let the person know your whereabouts. Place privacy controls on your social media to limit information you give out to the public.

In the early stages of dating someone, closely guard your identity and personal information. Instead of using your actual phone number, use a number from a texting app or Google Voice for calls. Don't reveal where you live and always meet in a public place. Avoid going over to each other's houses in the beginning. Don't disclose your income or personal traumas you've endured until you've gotten a better sense of someone's character. Don't loan money or let anyone move in with you before you know them very well. Sociopaths and psychopaths are always looking for people whose vulnerabilities they can exploit, those they can leech off of and con.

JOURNAL REFLECTION: **Know Your Predators**

Who are the toxic people and manipulators in your life? Make a list of people who exhibit the behaviors covered in this chapter. Next to each name, write down which of the five categories of toxicity they seem to most closely align with. Which of the strategies in this chapter can you practice next time you interact with each one of these people based on their category type?

Unlike more "tame" emotional vampires, boundary-steppers, and crazy-makers who have the capacity for empathy and change, malignant types are quite difficult to negotiate with and require an entirely different set of skills to safely tackle interactions with them. We'll dive more deeply into these in the next chapter.

CHAPTER THREE

Toxicity Playbook
Countering Manipulation Tactics

Even though it was many years ago, I still remember the night I walked into my local police precinct in Manhattan to get my first-ever restraining order at three a.m. I had just received another threatening message from my ex-boyfriend when I dialed 911. I filled out the police report carefully, my hand trembling and my heart beating what felt like a million times per minute. Thankfully, I had all the evidence I needed: I had documented the dozens of missed calls from anonymous phone numbers, the messages from fake email addresses, and the incessant texts he had sent every day to taunt me and try to ensnare me back into the relationship. He had even created a fake email address with my name with a reference to my books in it to remind me that he was always watching and that he would try to sabotage me. This wasn't surprising, considering he had subjected me to pathologically envious outbursts during the course of our relationship.

This time, I was prepared. In response to the barrage of messages that ranged from love bombing to rageful, I spoke to him calmly, stating only the facts, and told him to stop harassing me. When he continued to do so, I did not let him know I was calling the police. It took a day or so, but my ex-boyfriend was eventually arrested for his harassment, and I was granted a restraining order after he was released. After that, he never contacted me again.

Sadly, not all victims are so lucky. Many continue to be harassed and stalked by their partners years after they leave them. Some are even killed, and in some cases, restraining orders can worsen the situation.

In order to effectively tackle toxic people and narcissists, we have to be prepared. We have to learn the ins and outs of their behavior—why they do what they do, what their agenda is, and how we can react in ways that best protect us.

We briefly went over some of the behaviors toxic people use in chapter 1. As we address more of them in further detail here, keep in mind this distinction: The garden-variety types *occasionally* use these tactics to get what they want, some of them even unknowingly. But the malignant types use these manipulation techniques as *a way of life*. They employ them frequently and excessively, not only to achieve their agendas but also to provoke emotional reactions in others. Many of these tactics serve as diversionary methods to silence and belittle you. As you read over the stories that follow, see if you recognize some of these tactics and behaviors from your own relationship history.

Stonewalling and the Silent Treatment

Occasionally in a relationship, someone might want a "break" from an argument to cool off. When that happens, they communicate respectfully that this is what they need. Benign toxic types or more "avoidance-oriented" people may sometimes use *stonewalling*—an outright refusal to communicate—to avoid discussions that present a threat to the relationship (Kuster et al. 2017). With malignant types, however, it's drastically different. Narcissists use stonewalling in spades to emotionally invalidate and silence their victims. It's a way to cause their victims intense emotional pain, to one-up them and provoke them into losing control. According to researchers Kipling Williams and Steve Nida (2011), being socially ostracized or ignored—like being on the receiving end of stonewalling and the silent treatment—activates the *anterior cingulate cortex*, the same part of the brain that registers physical pain. Being shut down like this can be just as painful as getting punched in the face.

As a survivor, Lauren, described, "My narcissistic ex-boyfriend would retaliate by subjecting me to unreasonable and lengthy periods of the silent treatment, usually in response to me trying to express my emotions about something he did or said—or a boundary that he crossed. He went cold on me and disengaged from me when I found out that my father had been diagnosed with lung cancer."

The stonewaller does not allow you to have thoughts, opinions, or perceptions that differ from their own. They prefer to talk over you, shut you out, or cut off the lines of communication altogether. They invalidate your perspective and emotions, withdraw any kind of acknowledgment of your concerns, and issue ultimatums that coerce you into complying with their demands out of fear and obligation. Stonewalling causes victims to emotionally suppress and sacrifice their authentic emotions, which, according to research, lowers well-being and the quality of the relationship (Impett et al. 2012).

As researcher John Gottman discovered, stonewalling is one of the four communication styles in a relationship—the "four horsemen of the apocalypse," as he called them (1994)—that can predict its inevitable end; the others are defensiveness, contempt, and criticism, all of which also figure in the other manipulation tactics we'll discuss in this chapter.

In healthy relationships, *dyadic coping*, the process by which "one partner responds supportively to another person's stress signals by validating the partner's feelings, giving advice, or providing practical support," builds a stable foundation for the relationship (Kuster et al. 2017, 578). Dyadic coping is a reliable predictor of relationship quality, intimacy, and stability. When both partners are attuned to each other's needs, transparent and reciprocal in the way they validate each other's experiences, they feel safe in sharing their emotions and know they will be seen, heard, and supported. Shutting down conversations before they even begin is a surefire way to escape accountability and destroy intimacy and dyadic coping in a relationship.

This "demand-withdraw" pattern in relationships, where one person withdraws and the other becomes increasingly demanding and anxious in response, causes depression in the victims of stonewalling and further conflict in the relationship (Schrodt et al. 2013). While some partners (especially male partners) have a habit of using stone-walling to avoid conflict, what happens is that it actually causes *more* emotional tension and unresolved issues.

Stonewalling is even more powerful when it is callous, cold, and charged with manipulative intent. When malignant narcissists with-draw, they do so to make you beg for their approval. As psychologist Jeff Pipe, PsyD, writes, "In relationships, stonewalling is the emotional equivalent to cutting off someone's oxygen. The emotional detachment inherent to stonewalling is a form of abandonment" (2014). Stonewalling evokes initial feelings of terror, followed by feelings of anger and more futile efforts to get some reaction or resolution from the stonewaller. When these attempts fail, the person being stonewalled feels abandoned, uncared for, and unloved, as the following example of Lydia shows.

Lydia is concerned with the way her partner, John, has been treat-ing her. His temper has been out of control, and he has been relentlessly criticizing her. On her birthday, she attempts to bring up his behavior to him during dinner. In response, he invalidates her, telling her that she's overreacting. When she tries to explain how hurt she is by his recent remarks, he aggressively says, "I am done talking!" and abruptly leaves, exiting the apartment with no explanation and abandoning her on her birthday.

When Lydia tries to call him, he declines each of her phone calls and leaves her texts unread. Lydia tosses and turns all night, crying and worrying about him. He doesn't return. The productive conversation Lydia was hoping to have hasn't even had a chance to begin before it's already over, and what's more, John ruined her birthday. He calls the next day and acts as if nothing happened. When Lydia tries to ask John where he's been, he tells her, "You should really speak to a therapist about your issues" and hangs up on her without waiting for her response.

In this scenario, John yet again stonewalls her, emotionally invali-dates her, and rudely redirects the conversation, unwilling to address the issues at hand even as they continue to fester beneath the surface.

This causes more distress to Lydia and unnecessary tension and trauma, not to mention deep abandonment wounds. John is a typical narcissist in that he shows little to no empathy for Lydia's pain and abandons her on her special day. Had he actually taken the time to address her concerns (something he doesn't seem to have the emotional capacity to do), the outcome would've been far more productive and peaceful.

Although stonewalling seems to put an end to an ongoing conversation, it actually speaks volumes and communicates something quite cruel and belittling to the person on the receiving end. Regardless of the intention of the person doing the stonewalling, this behavior communicates to their partner: "You are insignificant. You're not worth responding to. Your thoughts and feelings don't matter to me. *You* don't matter to me."

A variation of stonewalling is the silent treatment. The silent treatment is a form of punishment and can be issued for no reason at all or to condition you to associate setting boundaries with devastating consequences. Manipulative predators often use the silent treatment to induce a sense of fear, obligation, and guilt in you so that you end up begging for their approval or acquiescing to what they want. Licensed mental health counselor Richard Zwolinski (2014) asserts that this tactic is a favorite of narcissists: "The silent treatment can be used as an abusive tactic that is the adult narcissist's version of a child's 'holding my breath until you give in and give me what I want.'"

If you've endured this type of manipulation, know that your feelings of abandonment are a normal reaction. Stonewalling and the silent treatment in the hands of a narcissist can be agonizing and excruciating.

Tips on Breaking Through Stonewalling and the Silent Treatment

When you're being given the silent treatment, use it as a period of freedom and self-care. Rather than reaching out to the person ignoring you, become mindful of your emotions and identify how this person is making you feel. Reframe the experience as an opportunity to detach from this person and as a reminder that you do not deserve this treatment. Remember that when a narcissist stonewalls you or subjects you to the silent treatment, they *want* you to respond. They want you to chase after them and plead for their attention. They want to provoke you. They want to control and diminish you.

If you're being stonewalled and have tried to communicate your feelings to no avail, realize that the problem is not you. If this is a chronic problem, you must step away from self-blame and stop walking on eggshells in an attempt to please someone who will not be pleased. A toxic person's communication patterns cannot be changed unless that person is willing to change them.

While stonewalling *can* be improved in healthier relationships where both people are willing to work to heal dysfunctional patterns, in an unhealthy relationship with a pathological partner, self-care and self-protection are paramount. There comes a time when it is far better to walk away and stop speaking to this person who is not interested in listening to you. Otherwise, you're just feeding into their sick mind games. When a narcissist stonewalls you, save your voice for people who actually respect you and engage in self-care.

JOURNAL REFLECTION: **Instances of Stonewalling**

Write down some instances when you've been shut down in a conversation. How did you feel? What were you unable to express? In the future, how can you take better care of yourself when you encounter stonewalling?

Gaslighting

Gaslighting is an insidious form of manipulation that aims to erode your sense of reality. When a toxic person gaslights you, they engage in crazy-making discussions in which they challenge and invalidate your thoughts, lived experiences, emotions, perceptions, and sanity. Gaslighting enables narcissists, sociopaths, and psychopaths to exhaust you to the point where you are unable to fight back. Rather than finding ways to healthily detach from this toxic person, you are sabotaged in your efforts to find a sense of certainty and validation in what you've experienced.

The term "gaslighting" first originated in Patrick Hamilton's 1938 *Gas Light*, a play about a manipulative husband who drives his wife to the brink of insanity by causing her to question her own reality. It was also popularized in the famous 1944 film adaptation, *Gaslight*, a psychological thriller about a man named Gregory Anton who murders a famous opera singer and later marries her niece, Paula.

Gregory messes with his wife's sense of reality by causing her to believe that her aunt's house is haunted so she can be institutionalized and he can gain access to the rest of her family jewels. He rearranges items in the house, flickers gaslights on and off, and makes disturbing noises in the attic. After manufacturing these crazy-making scenarios, he then convinces Paula that all these events are a figment of her imagination. He isolates her so that she is unable to seek support for the terror she is experiencing. He even recruits numerous third parties to reinforce this new false reality; for example, he brings in the maids to confirm that they did not a move a painting and convinces Paula that she was the one who must have moved it, even though she has no recollection of doing so. It is only when an outsider—an inspector—confirms to her that the gaslights are indeed flickering that she realizes she had been right all along.

This movie mirrors what many survivors go through when being covertly abused and isolated. They feel like they are losing their minds and cannot trust themselves. It is usually when they find an "inspector" of their own who validates their perceptions that they identify the elaborate attempts to undermine them.

The reason gaslighting is so effective is that the repetition of "alternative facts" alone can be powerful enough to dissuade us from holding on to our truth. Researchers discovered that when a statement is repeated multiple times (even when it is false and when subjects are *aware* that it is false), it is more likely to be rated as true simply due to the effect of repetition (Hasher, Goldstein, and Toppino 1977). This effect is even more powerful when the listener is tired or distracted by other information, as is often the case with victims of gaslighting when hit with the abuser's denials. Familiarity with a claim also plays a tremendous role in whether we believe it, sometimes even trumping credibility (Begg, Anas, and Farinacci 1992; Geraci and Rajaram 2016).

Manipulators who gaslight with the intention of rewriting history use this "illusory truth effect" to their advantage. They repeat falsehoods so often that they become instilled in the minds of their victims as irrefutable truths. Causing you to doubt your own reality, question the status of your mental health, and lose trust in your perceptions allows a manipulative person to get away with problematic behavior more easily. While they're busy rewriting history, you're too busy attempting to reconcile what you've seen, heard, and witnessed with the toxic person's claims to get a firm understanding of how your boundaries have been violated. It's common for malignant narcissists to gaslight their victims by saying things like, "I never said that," "You're overreacting," "You're oversensitive," or "You're blowing things way out of proportion."

Another common way narcissists gaslight their victims is by pathologizing them, behaving as if they are authoritative doctors diagnosing their unstable patients. Some domestic abusers go so far as to directly interfere with the mental health of their victims in order to concoct more evidence that the victim is "losing it." This weakens the credibility of their victims and depicts them as unstable or unhinged when they speak out against the abuse. In fact, the National Domestic Violence Hotline (NDVH) (2018) does not recommend couples therapy with an abuser, as therapy can be a space where victims are further violated and gaslighted. The NDVH, along with the National Center on Domestic Violence, Trauma, and Mental Health, estimate that 89 percent of its callers have experienced some form of mental health coercion from their abusers and that 43 percent have experienced substance abuse coercion (Warshaw et al. 2014). These abusers actively contributed to the mental health or substance use difficulties of their partners and then threatened to use this information against them in legal proceedings, such as child custody cases.

Everyday gaslighting can occur due to errors or misinterpretations, but deliberate gaslighting is executed with an agenda in mind. As therapist Stephanie Sarkis (2017) notes, malignant narcissists have a goal when it comes to gaslighting: "The goal is to make the victim or victims question their own reality and depend on the gaslighter. In the case of a person who has a personality disorder such as antisocial personality disorder, they are born with an insatiable need to control others."

Gaslighters use shaming, punishment, and emotional invalidation when their victims call out their abuse. Chronic gaslighting can cause an immense amount of fear, anxiety, self-doubt, and cognitive dissonance—that state of inner turmoil that arises due to contradictory and conflicting beliefs. On the one hand, the victim is noticing something that is amiss, not quite right. On the other, the victim feels blindsided by the gaslighter's authoritative and continual invalidation of their reality and perceptions, unable to trust their own experiences.

Victims of perpetual gaslighting walk on eggshells and come to rely on the gaslighter's falsehoods rather than their own perceptions. According to Robin Stern, PhD, author of *The Gaslight Effect* (2007), this is in part due to the victim's need for validation from the gaslighter, which is reinforced throughout the abuse cycle.

Katerina suspects that her husband, Dale, has been cheating on her. Not only is he coming home late from work, but he also often takes his phone with him to the bathroom, wakes up in the middle of the night to answer suspicious calls, and texts incessantly throughout dinner. Katerina has even discovered lingerie that does not belong to her in their bed, which Dale claims is hers. Each time Katerina tries to raise questions about where he has been and what he's been doing with whom, he pushes back, accusing her of imagining things, of being "crazy," "needy," and "paranoid." Despite the mounting evidence, she begins to wonder if she really *is* being paranoid. Perhaps the lingerie *was* hers, after all? Maybe the calls *were* to his colleagues, like he claimed. Maybe it really *is* her fault that he is distancing himself, as he's been telling her. Maybe he just needs time to himself, she reasons.

She begins avoiding confrontation with Dale altogether and tries her best to please him instead. She doubles her efforts to be a more loving, affectionate, and doting wife. She silences her lingering doubt, until one day she comes home early from work and finds him in bed with their next-door neighbor.

Tips on Dousing Gaslighting

If you suspect you're being gaslighted, enlist the help of a supportive third party, such as a trauma-informed therapist who specializes in recovery from this type of covert abuse. Work together to go through your narrative of what occurred in the relationship. Write down things as you experienced them to reconnect with your sense of reality. Keep a journal to record your emotions, thoughts, feelings, and perceptions— this way, you'll have an account of everything that's happened.

When in doubt, I'll remind you again to document everything, especially if you're encountering gaslighting in the workplace. You can print out emails, take screenshots of text messages, save voice mails, and, if legal in your state, record conversations. Rather than falling into the trap of wanting an explanation or validation from the gaslighter, turn to self-validation. When you reaffirm the reality of the abuse you've experienced, you'll get one step closer to healing from the narcissist. Anchor yourself in what happened and don't let anyone rewrite reality for you.

JOURNAL REFLECTION: Reality Check

Write down your story from *your* perspective, not the gaslighter's, to properly contextualize it. When you track your progress and narrate your reality in writing, you can identify recurring patterns of the abuser's long-standing behaviors rather than dismissing them as isolated incidents. You can then draw conclusions about the abuser's true character and agenda based on the rights that have been violated, confirming your experiences without subscribing to the gaslighter's claims. This helps relieve some of the self-blame and cognitive dissonance you've experienced as you work to rebuild self-trust. For example, a journal entry might look like this:

Example: *Jim called me terrible things today and insulted my appearance, even though I've asked him multiple times to stop being mean to me. It made me feel so degraded and small when he did it again without any apologies. When I called him out, he insisted I was being hypersensitive and that it was just a joke. But I've asked him many times to stop, and he's disrespected my wishes each and every time. He continues to verbally abuse me and disregard my feelings. It seems my feelings don't matter to him at all.*

The Cycle of Love Bombing, Premature Intimacy, and Devaluation

Love bombing is a manipulation method that cults use to groom their members. When it is done in a relationship with a narcissist or similar personality, you become part of a one-person cult. Love bombing involves excessive flattery, praise, and constant attention and affection showered on the target, usually in the beginning of a relationship, a friendship, or a work partnership, to get the victim heavily invested in the relationship early on. The higher the investment, the more difficult it can be for the victim to detach even once the manipulator reveals their true colors.

As survivor Danielle recalled, "When we first started dating, it was like I knew him forever. We talked for hours. Our interests were similar and our hobbies were as well. After a short period of dating, he told me he loved me via text—that I was his soul mate and he was going to marry me one day. I felt rushed, but I was afraid to lose such a good, hardworking family man."

Love bombing targets our greatest vulnerabilities and desires: to be seen, heard, noticed, validated, and cherished. It is the gateway drug to addiction with a narcissistic partner. Narcissists use it to get us biochemically bonded to them and to disclose our personal information early on so they can better manipulate us. And this strategy works!

Arthur Aron and his fellow researchers (1997) discovered that intimacy between two strangers could be heightened by having them ask each other a series of increasingly personal questions; a close bond was created by "sustained, escalating, reciprocal, personal self-disclosure."

With a narcissist, considerable time is spent on this type of "premature intimacy" in the early stages of a relationship. They often disclose seemingly personal things about themselves (whether fabricated or truthful) to get us comfortable with sharing our deepest desires with them. Based on the information they gather from us, they construct a mask filled with the same qualities we long for in a partner—to make us feel like we're experiencing a once-in-a-lifetime connection. Through the practice of *future-faking*, they dangle the carrot of a promised future, discussing marriage, children, and a life together at the onset of the relationship. We then invest blindly in a future that may never actually come to fruition. We put our time, energy, and finances into a con artist whose promises are empty.

Love bombing is incredibly powerful when it is used on someone who is still healing from a loss or a trauma or someone with some kind of void in their lives. As Dale Archer, MD, explains, "The dopamine rush of the new romance is vastly more powerful than it would be if the target had a healthy self-image, because the love bomber fills a need the target can't fill on her own" (2017).

Once victims are sufficiently hooked, toxic people then push them off the pedestal. This is known as *devaluation*. Periodically, they still give their victims "scraps" of the idealization phase, causing victims to work even harder to regain the honeymoon phase of the relationship. Psychologists call this *intermittent reinforcement* of positive rewards to provoke a response in the victim (see below for a fuller discussion of this form of reinforcement). Whenever the victim is about to leave, the abuser swoops in with the "nice guy" or "nice girl" act, causing victims to doubt themselves and the true nature of their abusers. HSPs fall victim to love bombing because they are so heavily emotional themselves that they resonate with the depth of interest shown to them by predators.

Tips to Defuse Love Bombing

When excessive flattery is given at the beginning of any relationship, mark it as suspect. Remember that you're still getting to know this person and that any praise you are given is superficial, even if it is accurate. You can still politely accept compliments without investing in someone you do not know. Organic partnerships will be built over time with consistent levels of respect and evidence of trustworthiness, not a frenzied display of unwarranted amounts of interest. Work on your own sense of self-worth, self-love, and self-esteem so you don't feel as easily swayed by someone sweeping you off your feet.

Slow down the relationship, avoid physical intimacy in the first stages of dating, and observe how the other person reacts to your boundaries. Do they respect your boundaries, or do they engage in *fast-forwarding*, pushing and coercing you to move faster than you'd like, becoming enraged and controlling? These are red flags. Trust genuine connection that builds over time rather than instantaneous chemistry. When someone love bombs you, don't respond by overinvesting or matching their level of interest. Instead, see it as an indication that they must prove their empty words with their actions and consistent behaviors over time. Love bomb *yourself* with self-esteem and slow down the pace of the relationship. Know your self-worth so you don't need other people to feed you accolades.

JOURNAL REFLECTION: **Halt Love Bombing**

Reflect on a toxic person who has love bombed you or is love bombing you now. How can you slow down the relationship? If this was a past relationship, what action could you have taken to keep more of a distance? Options include: not responding to constant texts, taking a break from seeing each other during the week, and slowing down the pace of physical intimacy.

Intermittent Reinforcement

Intermittent reinforcement in the context of an abusive relationship is used to manipulate victims into working harder for their abuser's approval. Psychologists Charles Ferster and B. F. Skinner (1957) discovered that animals are more likely to respond to a stimulus when its rewards are unpredictable or on an "intermittent reinforcement" schedule. For example, a rat presses a lever more fervently and persistently when it is taught that the reward comes randomly, rather than predictably whenever it is pushed. Similarly, a gambler at a slot machine will keep playing in the hopes of a win despite the losses to get the rare reward. Bottom line? We work harder for what we can't seem to have or even the evasive hope of obtaining it like we did once before. As we learned in the beginning of this book, intermittent reinforcement is particularly powerful in creating a biochemical bond with a toxic partner.

Those on the narcissistic spectrum know this instinctively and use intermittent reinforcement against the people they target. When they've locked a victim into an abuse cycle, they still throw in scraps of affection, attention, love bombing, and bits of the honeymoon phase to keep their victims on their toes. This ensures the victim is always working harder to regain the approval of the narcissist, rather than brainstorming ways to *get out* of the toxic relationship. If an abuser was consistently mean, the victim would have no reason to stay.

However, this display of intermittent affection feeds what clinical psychologist Joe Carver (2014) calls the "small kindness perception." As victims, we perceive any kind of affectionate action or words after enduring agonizing abuse in a more amplified manner. Even a period of *no abuse* can count as "affection" in our eyes because the absence of terror is perceived as a gift to those who are accustomed to a war zone. Much like a small crumb feels like a loaf of bread to a starving person, an abused victim sees the occasional kind deed as evidence of their abuser's generosity and mistakes it for the totality of their character rather than a tactic embedded within the abuse cycle. This gives victims false hope that their abusers will change.

Terry's wife, Michelle, was incredibly abusive. She would throw things at him, scream at him, and frequently threaten to take their children away. Terry came to anticipate and fear her rage attacks whenever he came home. Her behavior was unpredictable and volatile. Most of the time, she was angry and sullen. Yet there were also days when she seemed calm. On those rare days, she would cook him a lavish meal, shower him with affection, and talk excitedly about future plans. He savored those nights of peace and felt especially bonded to Michelle then; it reminded him of when they first met—how charming she had been and how they would spend hours talking into the early dawn.

Unfortunately, the next day, her abusive behavior would return like clockwork. Despite Michelle's dangerous behavior, Terry still felt attached to her; he was convinced they had a once-in-a-lifetime kind of connection. After all, when it was good, it was *really* good; when it was bad, it was really bad. He rationalized that he would have to accept the bad times in order to get to the good. This is a common way abusers use intermittent reinforcement of positive behaviors to keep their victims trauma-bonded to them and the abuse cycle.

Tips on Tackling Intermittent Reinforcement

When you notice a cycle of hot-and-cold behavior, press pause and withdraw from the interaction. Do not feed this cycle by responding positively to a person who finally returns to "good" behavior after a period of toxicity. If good behavior from someone you know is "shocking" and a relief to you, consider this a red flag rather than a green light to keep moving forward with the relationship.

Instead of entertaining inconsistent behavior, *make your own behavior consistent* by detaching from someone who disrespects you. Depending on the circumstances, you can cut ties with this person completely or do a slow "fade" from their life. Abusive individuals to whom you've given second, third, and fourth chances do not deserve any more chances. Abort the mission of attempting to change them.

They have shown you time and time again that they will not change, and even if they *do* appear to change, remember that they are just temporarily morphing into the person they were in the beginning—to get you to trust them again in order to exploit you. Do not fall for it. See the cycle for what it is: an endless loop that will always return to its toxic beginnings. When someone goes hot and cold, it's time for you to go cold for good.

JOURNAL REFLECTION: **Curb the Conditioning**

Write down some instances of hot-and-cold behavior you've experienced. How did you react when the person went cold (example: *I called them multiple times trying to get their attention, but they never responded*)? How will you react in the future (example: *I will withdraw from interacting with them and spend time with someone who cares about me or doing something I care about*)?

Hoovering

When toxic people are met with boundaries or the ending of a relationship, some continue to test these boundaries long after the expiration date of the relationship by repeated attempts to contact you. They reach out to suck you back into the traumatic vortex of the relationship like a Hoover vacuum, which is why this tactic is known as "hoovering."

Hoovering allows toxic people to "check in" with their targets when they are moving forward with their lives. For example, an abusive ex-partner might hoover their victim by sending them texts on certain holidays reminiscing about the happy moments they had together. A toxic mother might hoover her adult daughter by calling her after giving her the silent treatment. A garden-variety jerk might hoover by reaching out to one of the girls he "played" in hopes that she'll be receptive to reconciliation. Hoovering can also be indirectly staged through third parties who "pass on" the abuser's message or through social media stalking. It can consist of love bombing messages, stories about how they've magically changed (they haven't), devaluing or provocative messages, a fabricated emergency or illness, or, even more sadistically, messages that brag about the abuser's new partner.

Contrary to popular myth, when the person doing the reaching out is toxic, hoovering is not about missing someone or loving them. Researchers Justin Mogilski and Lisa Welling (2017) discovered that those who had darker personality traits such as narcissism, psychopathy, and duplicity made attempts to stay friends with their exes out of pragmatism, sex, and for access to the person's resources—*not* because they missed or loved them or had any kind of epiphany about their destructive behavior toward others. So if you're met with a "friend request" from a toxic ex-partner whether online or in real life, be wary. Their intentions are likely not as pure as you might assume.

Licensed psychologist Tony Ferretti notes, "Narcissists hate to fail or lose, so they will do what they can to maintain some connection if they didn't make the choice to end it.… [T]hey may stay connected [to exes in order to] have access to valuable resources. They also have inside information about their exes' vulnerabilities and weaknesses that they can exploit and manipulate, which gives them a sense of power and control" (Tourjée 2016).

Narcissists are not above publishing provocative posts on their online platforms to try to get a rise out of their victims, and digital platforms have made it technologically speedy for them to hoover, stalk, and harass their victims with more ferocity. In the olden days, toxic people would've had to send smoke signals and write letters to hoover you; now they make use of Facebook, Instagram, Twitter, and Snapchat, create multiple phone numbers using apps, and even install spyware on the devices of their victims.

Hoovering gets your hopes up that "this time will be different," preventing you from reestablishing full control over your life and remaining entangled in the narcissist's toxic web. In the mind of the narcissistic individual, if they can "bait" you to respond and engage with them, they can also bait you back into the relationship.

Tips on How to Intercept Hoovering

To prevent hoovering, block the toxic person's number, email, and all their social media profiles. Cut off ties with any mutual friends they may use to spy on you, whether online or in real life. Of course, the narcissist may still try to hoover through other means, like through anonymous accounts or by stalking (in which case, you'll want to document these attempts and report to law enforcement depending on the circumstances).

When this occurs, do not give in to the hoovering. Reframe your automatic assumption that an attempt to reestablish contact in any way means that the toxic person misses you; rather, say to yourself, "They don't miss *me*. They miss controlling me." Write down a list of abusive incidents to ground yourself back into the reality of the abuse and mistreatment you experienced (work with a counselor to do this if you find it triggering). This will reconnect you to the reality of the situation rather than false promises or fantasies. Make a habit of anchoring yourself like this when hoovered.

If for some reason you have to respond, minimize harm as much as possible. For example, with a work colleague you can't avoid interacting with or an ex-partner you co-parent with, stick to the facts and keep it simple. Remain as emotionally unreactive as possible to their tactics. If your abusive father texts you to ask if you're coming to Thanksgiving dinner, let him know you won't be able to make it *without* going into the details and giving in to his attempts at emotional blackmail or guilt-tripping. If a slimy ex writes loving posts about their new partner and texts you about how happy they are, document the texts in case you need evidence of their harassment; block their number and social media accounts. Remember, a "no" is not a negotiation or an invitation to be persuaded. When hoovered, don't get sucked back in. Block, document, and delete.

Don't Get Sucked into the Toxic Vortex

On which platforms and media do you have contact with a toxic person? How can you prevent them from accessing you and protect your privacy or decrease the chance of being hoovered? For example, in co-parenting situations, you might use a third-party application such as Our Family Wizard, which allows you to communicate through a system that documents interactions for the court. On social media, you can block the toxic person and restrict your settings so no revealing information is accessible to the public. If you're being stalked or harassed, log these instances whenever possible should you ever decide to take legal action.

Toxic Shaming

When toxic people can't manipulate you, they resort to unhealthy shaming in order to instill a sense of fear, obligation, and guilt about you being an independent person with different opinions, preferences, needs, and desires. Chronic shaming lowers our self-esteem. Research indicates that both men and women who have their self-esteem lowered are more agreeable and compliant to the requests of others (Walster 1965; Gudjonsson and Sigurdsson 2003). So when a toxic person or a narcissist shames and judges you excessively for not fulfilling their desires, there's a chance that you may actually scramble to try to meet their demands.

Shaming also works because it taps into the core wounds of childhood, reawakening what trauma therapists call the "inner critic" (Walker 2013). In his book *Homecoming*, psychologist John Bradshaw distinguishes between healthy shame and toxic shame. Whereas healthy shame reminds us of our limitations, "toxic shame forces us to be more than human (perfect) or less than human" (1990, 199). As adults, when we are shamed by toxic people, we feel guilty, even when the accusation is without merit, and we regress back to powerful childhood emotions and beliefs.

Jared's brother, Ben, consistently tried to get his brother to loan him money. Whenever Jared tried to set boundaries by telling his brother he couldn't give him a loan, Ben would shame him. "You're so stingy—always spending money on yourself," he would remark whenever Jared bought something for himself like a new pair of shoes, even though just the week before, Jared had spent a considerable amount helping to pay Ben's bills. This was a manipulative accusation meant to make Jared feel guilty about setting boundaries and had no basis in reality.

Toxic people use shaming remarks because they can make us feel as if *we* are the problem, when in reality, it's the toxic person's own dysfunction that causes them to excessively judge and criticize others. As HSPs, we internalize this form of shaming because we are so attuned to the emotions of others and are highly conscientious about how we make others feel. Unhealthy shaming and judgment from others affects us deeply, especially if we grew up in abusive households where we were taught that our worth was tied to gaining approval and pleasing others.

Tips on How to Shun Shaming

When you are being shamed by a toxic person, mindfully resist internalizing that shame. Breathe through your automatic impulse to absorb the shame like a sponge and, instead, figuratively "hand" the shame back to the person shaming you. Mentally say to yourself, *This doesn't belong to me. This is yours.* Resist the compulsion to try to gain this person's approval or cater to their needs. Instead, acknowledge when you might be having an *emotional flashback* (a regression back into childhood wounds and emotions) and use this as an opportunity to do some inner work to heal those wounds.

Show yourself compassion when healing these wounds. Clinical psychologist Tara Brach (2020) created the excellent acronym RAIN to help you do so: *Recognize* what is happening; *allow* life to be just as it is; *investigate* with gentle attention; and *nurture*. You may hold a hand to your heart or cheek when saying affirmations such as, "I love you. You didn't deserve the horrible things that happened to you. You deserve the very best. I am sorry you went through this. I am here for you. I accept you. I approve of you." Giving yourself approval, validation, affection, attention, and love builds a healthy barrier between you and the toxic shaming tactics of others. It also eases the burden of any self-blame you may be experiencing from old wounds. Replace shame with self-compassion.

JOURNAL REFLECTION: **Speaking to Your Inner Child**

Write about the first times you felt shamed as a child. If you feel too triggered, go through this exercise with a counselor. As you remember these times, visualize yourself as a child—innocent and helpless. Send love and compassion to this child. Speak to the child kindly and let them know that you are there for them whenever they need it and that they don't need to be ashamed anymore. Remind them that they did not deserve the mistreatment they endured—they were an innocent victim of circumstance.

Projection

Toxic people displace their own shortcomings and issues onto others; this is a defense mechanism called *projection*. Much like an individual's shaming tactics have more to do with their own sense of shame, projections are a way for toxic people to escape responsibility for their own negative behavior and traits, as they dump their traits and behaviors onto others. While we all engage in projection to some extent, narcissistic personality clinical expert Linda Martinez-Lewi, PhD, asserts that the projections of a narcissist are often psychologically abusive. Narcissists use malignant projections to deliberately terrorize their victims and to cast their victims as the perpetrators. As Martinez-Lewi (2018) writes, "With constant ugly primitive projections of volcanic rage, humiliations, withering criticisms, the covert narcissist creates a horrendous, nightmarish environment for his [or her] spouse. The partner or spouse of the covert narcissist survives in a state of constant psychological and emotional siege."

In the twisted world of the narcissist's distorted insults, it is always "opposite day." Narcissists call intelligent and successful people lazy or moronic and accuse them of being full of themselves (quite an ironic projection given the narcissist's own egocentrism and cockiness). They verbally abuse their partners and call beautiful, successful people unattractive and unappealing. They claim loving, compassionate, and empathetic people are monsters. They accuse loyal people of deception and infidelity. They convince you that you are the opposite of what you really are: a kind, beautiful, intelligent, successful, and compassionate human being. A narcissist's malignant projections have nothing to do with you and *everything* to do with them. Listen closely—what they see in you is actually what they fail to notice about themselves in the mirror.

Priyanka's sociopathic boyfriend, Nathan, accused her of cheating on him, even though he was the one having multiple affairs behind her back. He would regularly check her phone for "clues" that she was talking to other guys and show up unannounced to her house to "catch her in the act." Their relationship eventually ended when Priyanka discovered that Nathan had numerous online dating profiles and was having unprotected sex with five different girls.

George had a narcissistic boss who was always accusing him of being unoriginal and uncreative. When George would share his ideas in meetings, his boss would criticize him for not being more innovative, only to later steal George's ideas and call them his own. It was eventually discovered that this same boss had ripped off the ideas of numerous other employees and took credit for them.

Beth's roommate, Chelsea, was a crazy-maker—she was constantly starting arguments over irrelevant things and would often come home belligerent and drunk. When Beth told her roommate politely that she could no longer handle the stress of their living arrangements and wanted her to move out, Chelsea accused Beth of being a "drama queen."

Tips on Pushing Away Projection

When met with a projection by a toxic person, imagine that they are actually saying this same thing about themselves and reject that projection. For example, when your narcissistic ex-partner tells you what a terrible parent you are, realize that they are actually talking about themselves—*they* are the terrible parent. When your toxic friend judges you for being single, realize that they are projecting their unhappiness of their own relationship onto you. You don't have to accept anyone's projections. See the projection for what it is and figuratively hand it back when you begin ruminating over the insults.

Mentally translate what the narcissist is really saying, especially if they are pathologically envious of you. Do not tell the narcissist your translation directly, as it will likely induce their rage—this is simply an exercise for *you*. For instance, if a narcissist told you, "You always overreact! You're so bitter and hateful!" remember how they lash out in rage over the smallest perceived slight. Who's *actually* the one that overreacts? Who is *truly* the "bitter and hateful" person? You can also mentally translate what the narcissist says into what they really mean. If they belittle your success, for example, you might translate this to: "I am jealous of what you've accomplished. It threatens my sense of superiority. I have to make you feel small in order to feel better about myself."

Here are a few other specific ways you can overcome projection.

Collect evidence that challenges projections. Remember the feedback you've received from other empathic people. Our brains tend to hang on to negativity more than positivity—they are accustomed to look for danger in order to combat threats in our environment to survive. And because we react more strongly to negativity, we are more deeply affected by it as a result. As Roy Baumeister and his fellow researchers note, "Bad emotions, bad parents and bad feedback have more impact than good ones.... Put another way, you are more upset about losing $50 than you are happy about gaining $50" (Baumeister et al. 2001, 323–326). Researchers Andrew Newberg, MD, and Mark

Waldman (2013) note that even a single negative word can increase activity in the amygdala, the center for fear and anxiety. It's important to balance the emotional seesaw. There is likely far more evidence to the contrary that you are not considering because your "survival brain" is latching onto the narcissist's negativity as truth. Recall and document healthy feedback and facts that contradict the narcissist's projections. *This is for you, not the narcissist.*

Write down a list of accomplishments, compliments, and facts that refute the narcissist's faulty distortion. Create an audiotape reminiscing about all the things you're proud of. Make a bulletin board of photographs that capture joyful moments in your life. Save screenshots of sweet texts, emails, social media comments, and more that can serve as anchors to remind you of who you truly are and what you're capable of. Refer to these repetitively whenever you feel self-doubt. By mentally savoring compliments, accomplishments, and positive experiences, we reject the narcissist's vile accusations as gospel. Recondition yourself to remember positive feedback rather than the narcissist's pathologically envious projections.

Retrain your subconscious mind so you can self-validate and channel your pain into success. Meditation, positive affirmations, and hypnosis can do wonders for reworking the destructive falsehoods the narcissist has taught you to believe about yourself. Research shows the positive impact these healing modalities have on emotion regulation, coping with anxiety, and sense of self-worth (Lazar et al. 2011; Cascio et al. 2015; Jiang et al. 2017; Kaiser et al. 2018). We'll learn more about healing modalities in the final chapter of this book. You can use what the narcissist has degraded in you as an incentive to prove them wrong by working on rebuilding your life, goals, and dreams. Once you learn to self-validate and channel the pain of what was done to you into your highest good and the greater good, you can successfully overcome the narcissist's malignant projections.

If you *need* to respond to a narcissist's projection in a situation where interactions are unavoidable, do so succinctly. Calmly say something like,

"That actually describes you more than me" before exiting the conversation. Just know that narcissists are unlikely to admit that their projections are more about them than you. That's why your time is better spent validating yourself and seeing the projection for what it is: an attempt by the narcissist to make you a trash receptacle for their problems.

JOURNAL REFLECTION: **Translating Toxic Projections**

Write down an insult you've been given by a toxic person. Next, write down the translation—the projection the narcissist is trying to hand over to you. Then, note the behavior and attitude shift you can implement as a result of this translation. For example:

1. **The narcissist told me:** "You're so full of yourself. You're so selfish!"

2. **The translation:** "I am so full of myself and selfish. I can't stand to see you be confident and set boundaries because it takes the control, power, and attention away from me, so I'd rather guilt you for doing this."

3. **Behavior shift:** Now that I know the narcissistic person is trying to guilt me into not setting boundaries or building confidence, I have even more incentive to do so.

Do as many of these as you can and see how it changes your perspective on the narcissist's insults and reveals their hidden motives.

Hypercriticism, Nitpicking, and Moving the Goalposts

One of the ways manipulative predators control us is through *hypercriticism*—heavily scrutinizing anything and everything we do. This includes casting hypercritical remarks about our appearance, personality, lifestyle, achievements, talents, work ethic, choices, and more. Everything is fair game in a narcissist's mind. Shaming us for existing as an independent human being with our own preferences, opinions, and worldviews is the way narcissists program us to self-destruct. In an interview for CTV News, clinical psychologist Simon Sherry noted that hypercriticism is a form of narcissistic perfectionism that is "corrosive" and destructive to other people: "The criticism is ceaseless. And if you fall short of their lofty standards, they're likely to lash out at you in a harsh way" (MacDonald and Sherry 2016).

Hypercriticism is the weapon with which narcissists commit emotional murder with clean hands. Yet narcissists themselves often fall far below the high standards they set for others. If we are subconsciously trained to view ourselves through the narcissist's hypercritical lens, we are unable to feel a steady sense of self-worth and rejoice in our accomplishments. This gives them the power to shape our self-perception, self-esteem, and self-efficacy. For example, a narcissistic mother who constantly nitpicks her daughter's weight may cause her to struggle with self-harm and eating disorders in adulthood. Hypercriticism can even lead to suicidal ideation, especially if we endured it at an early age during a vulnerable developmental stage.

Constructive criticism is (usually) given to *help* you; destructive criticism is used to dismantle your sense of self. Perhaps the greatest distinction between constructive and destructive criticism is the presence of personal attacks and impossible standards. Destructive critics don't want to help you improve; they want to rig the game and set you up to fail. They want an excuse to nitpick, pull you down, and scapegoat you in any way they can.

Toxic people use the tactic of "moving the goalposts" to ensure that they have every reason to be endlessly dissatisfied with you, regardless of what you do or don't do for them. Even after you've done everything in the world to satisfy their arbitrary desires, provided all the evidence to validate your perspective, or taken every action to meet their request, they set up yet another expectation of you, demand more proof, or get you to meet yet another goal. These goalposts will continually change and may even be unrelated; they don't have any other point besides making you work harder for the narcissist's approval.

By raising expectations higher and higher each time or switching them abruptly, toxic people instill in you a pervasive sense of unworthiness, of never feeling quite "enough." By rehashing one irrelevant fact or hyperfocusing on what you did wrong, narcissists divert away from your strengths and accomplishments and toward your fabricated flaws. They pull you into obsessing over any weaknesses instead and worrying over the next demand of theirs you're going to have to meet, until, eventually, you've bent over backward trying to fulfill their every need, only to realize none of it changed the horrific ways they've mistreated you.

Tips on Moving Past the Goalposts and into Self-Acceptance

The antidote to moving goalposts is self-validation—developing a sense of being worthy and enough from within, knowing you do not have to prove yourself to anyone who attempts to belittle you. If you find yourself being asked to prove yourself constantly, recognize this as a red flag for manipulation. Don't get sucked into nitpicking comments and changing goalposts; if someone refuses to acknowledge the work you've done to validate your point or to satisfy them, remember that their motive isn't to better understand you or to provide feedback on how you can improve. It's to further provoke you as they position themselves as a superior figure. Validate and approve of yourself. In more or less words, let the toxic person know, "I've already met that expectation. I am not interested in trying to further prove myself to you."

Here are some more things you can do:

- Work with a counselor to reprogram your negative belief systems.

- Use hypnotherapy as a supplemental tool to instill new, healthier beliefs.

- Create an inventory of all of the compliments and kind words you've heard throughout your lifetime, especially related to the very things that the toxic person insulted. This list will help you realize how much support you do have from genuine, healthy people. It reminds you that the toxic person has an agenda when they insult you—one of keeping you down. Moving past the goalposts and into self-acceptance requires raising yourself up.

• Make a list of positive affirmations you can say to yourself daily, tailored to soothing your doubts and insecurities. Record them on your phone or a tape recorder. Hearing them said aloud in your own voice, or even in the voice of a loved one as suggested by self-help author Louise Hay, can be especially powerful in reworking your self-perception and curbing your negative self-talk. This dampens the force of that internalized critic who developed out of the narcissist's demeaning comments.

Know that you don't deserve to feel constantly deficient or unworthy in some way—whether in the workplace or in a romantic relationship. Don't keep up with the moving goalposts. Get centered in your own self-worth. You are already enough.

JOURNAL REFLECTION: **Affirmations to Counter Criticism**
Write down some affirmations you can tell yourself whenever a rumination over a criticism arises. For example, if you're remembering a time a toxic person scrutinized your appearance, you may have an affirmation like "I am beautiful inside and out" to replace this rumination every time it comes up. This will reprogram your mind over time to believe in the affirmation rather than the rumination.

Destructive Conditioning

Toxic people respond to your strengths, talents, and happy memories with abuse, frustration, and disrespect. They use what I call "destructive conditioning" to get you to associate your happiest moments, interests, passions, and dreams with their cruel and callous punishment. This is a form of what psychologists call *positive punishment*—the addition of aversive consequences to prevent your goal-directed behavior. As you are repeatedly punished for achieving, you begin a pattern of *negative reinforcement*, where you avoid the very goals that you have been conditioned to associate with the narcissist's punishment to gain a sense of safety or relief from their backlash. Like Pavlov's dogs, you're "trained" over time to become afraid of doing the very things that once made your life happy and fulfilling, all while being isolated from your friends and family which makes you emotionally and financially dependent on the toxic person.

Once the honeymoon phase is over, they will covertly and overtly put down the qualities and traits they once idealized. They will kick you off the pedestal they created and devalue you. They will ruin holidays, vacations, birthdays, anniversaries, and special occasions.

Narcissists destructively condition us by dampening our enthusiasm and raining on our parade during moments when we should be rejoicing, such as the birth of a child or a recent business success. This interferes with what relationship researchers term *capitalization*—the expression of excitement for experiences or accomplishments that enhances the perceived value of those experiences (Reis et al. 2010). When we are unable to share exciting news with a partner without being punished or belittled, it deflates our enjoyment of what should be a celebration. Detracting from any kind of milestone or achievement to divert the focus back to the narcissist is an indication of their pathological need to be the center of attention at all times. Take a look at what some real-life survivors experienced during what should have been the happiest moments of their lives:

Brooke: "*My father has sabotaged every celebration in my life
and made it about him. Every graduation from high school,
college, and even graduate school, my baby shower, and my child's
blessing ceremony.*"

Amanda: "*Every holiday, my mother makes up an excuse to be angry at us so we look like terrible children who leave her alone on the holidays. She didn't show up at my high school graduation. She told me my baby shower was tacky and I had to beg her to show up. She threw huge fits at both of our weddings and threatened to leave in the middle of them. The list goes on and on. We are not allowed to be happy or have a moment that is ours.*"

Megan: "*When I became engaged, my stepmother went out and bought a two-carat diamond ring for herself because I was excited that I had my engagement ring and people were paying attention to me. I had mentioned that my dream car would be a hunter green Jeep Grand Cherokee. A week later, she also bought my dream car.*"

Rachael: "*Every single holiday or important day has been ruined by one of my husband's tantrums or nasty comments. Every single one. I was called a horrible name on Mother's Day, had gifts thrown at me at Christmastime for accidentally opening a package that was addressed to him, called names for not wanting to hike down a steep cliff to the beach at night with no light—and that is just the beginning.*"

Narcissists seek to destroy anything that threatens their control over your life; they are pathologically envious and don't want anything to come in between them and their influence over you. After all, if you learn that you can get validation, respect, and love from other sources besides them, what's to keep you from leaving? To malignant toxic people, a little conditioning can go a long way to keep you walking on eggshells and falling short of your big dreams.

Destructive conditioning instills in us a sense of learned hopelessness. It causes us to struggle with a pervasive sense of fear that whenever things in our life are going well, our toxic parent, partner, sibling, friend, coworker, or boss could come around and attempt to rob us of it.

Destructive conditioning makes us feel that anything we derive joy from can be minimized, tainted in some fundamental way, or even taken away from us entirely for an unjust reason.

Tips on Curbing Destructive Conditioning

Extinction of our destructively conditioned responses can occur when we are able to confront the fear of achieving by repeatedly engaging in goal-directed behavior without the presence of the narcissist's punishment. Make a list of past successes, accomplishments, happy moments, and any other sources of joy that have been tainted by a narcissistic abuser. Write down how they sabotaged you, how you felt, and the aftermath of experiencing this sabotage. Then brainstorm ways in which you can reconnect to that source of joy independently of the narcissist. Here are some examples:

- If your narcissistic friend always degraded your dream career, think about ways you can pursue that goal anyway.

- If your toxic parent always rained on your birthday celebrations, start a habit of inviting only friends and relatives who are supportive of you to join you on your special day.

- Avoid telling narcissistic individuals about upcoming happy events or recent successes.

- Honor your accomplishments frequently by holding special ceremonies and gatherings that do not include the toxic person.

Recondition yourself to associate a healthy sense of pride and exhilaration with the passions, hobbies, interests, aspirations, and achievements the narcissist diminished in you. You deserve to feel the full range of joy for what you've accomplished. Don't let pathological envy steal what is rightfully yours.

JOURNAL REFLECTION: **Honor Your Accomplishments**

Write down three things you are proud of. It might be helpful to note three each in the following areas:

- Professional and academic
- Social life
- Self-development
- Parenting/other relationship responsibilities
- Fitness/health
- Mental health

Next to each, list the ways you have celebrated that accomplishment and brainstorm at least one way you can celebrate it now and reward yourself.

Smear Campaigns

Covert predators spread falsehoods to slander your reputation and degrade your credibility to others. A *smear campaign* is a preemptive strike to sabotage you so that you won't have a support network to fall back on lest you decide to detach and cut ties with the toxic person. They may gossip behind your back, slander you to their or your loved ones, create stories that depict you as the abuser while they play the victim, and claim that you engaged in the same behaviors that they are afraid *you* will accuse them of engaging in. They can tell blatant lies, rumors, or faux-concerned "suggestions" that call into doubt your sanity and character; they can even resort to manufacturing false evidence. They will also methodically, covertly, and deliberately provoke you so they can use your emotional reactions to the abuse as proof of your instability.

This is a form of gaslighting designed to manage your image in the public eye to ensure that no one will believe you're being abused. When toxic types can't control the way you see yourself, they start to control how others see you; they play the martyr and victim while you're labeled the toxic one. Abusers work overtime to paint *you* as the abuser in order to escape accountability for their actions. They may even stalk and harass you or the people you know as a way to supposedly "expose" the truth about you; this exposure acts as a way to hide their own abusive behavior while projecting it onto you. Some smear campaigns can even pit two people or two groups against each other. A victim in an abusive relationship often doesn't know what's being said about them during the relationship, but they eventually uncover the falsehoods.

Smear campaigns can be launched in romantic relationships, at the workplace, amid friendship circles, through the media, and within extended families. It's not uncommon for a pathologically envious, sociopathic coworker to feed misinformation about their hardworking colleagues to their bosses in order to eliminate them as a "threat" when climbing the corporate ladder. When narcissists infiltrate the higher ranks of authority and power, they have the potential to cause even more devastation by sabotaging those they perceive as competition. As Joe Navarro, former FBI profiler, writes in his book *Dangerous Personalities*, "Narcissism can reach high levels in high-powered or high-trust professions, where transgressions and abuses of authority can have devastating consequences" (2017, 41). The more authority someone possesses, the more devastating a smear campaign launched against a victim can be. Smear campaigns can create long-lasting damage.

Tips When Encountering Smear Campaigns

If you are being met with any kind of smear campaign or slander, continue to stick to the truth and let your integrity and character speak for themselves. Present *only the facts* if you are met with unwarranted accusations. The best "revenge" is living your own life, rebuilding your social networks with trustworthy people, and moving forward into success. Let go of the people who choose to support the narcissist; they will find out how wrong they are on their own. It's not your job to convince them. Take it as a blessing that you now know who your true friends are.

As difficult as it is, try not to become emotionally responsive in public—narcissists will use your emotional reactions against you to further depict you as the "crazy" one. Focus on any legal consequences you can take against a smear campaign; carefully document evidence of abuse whenever possible if you need to build a case. Research the defamation laws in your state and, if necessary, enlist the help of a lawyer who is familiar with high-conflict personalities.

Create a healthy support network that encourages you during difficult times—ideally, one that includes a trauma-informed therapist who understands personality disorders and other survivors who have been where you are. This support network should consist of authentic, trustworthy people who have your back—*not* those who enable or support the toxic person in your life. The last thing you need is to be further gaslighted, invalidated, or retraumatized when you are enduring a smear campaign.

Some readers have asked me, "Is it worth going out of my way to expose the narcissist to the public?" Typically, trying to bring down a psychopath single-handedly can be a dangerous endeavor, and I *highly* recommend that you prioritize your own sense of safety above all else and consult a lawyer and mental health professional to thoroughly discuss your individual case. Exposing someone publicly can come with potential consequences, and malignant toxic people are likely to retaliate by accusing *you* of character defamation—even if everything you've said is true. Remember, these types tend to be charming and supported by society. While garden-variety toxic people fear exposure and will inevitably back off at the potential of it, psychopathic individuals are incredibly ruthless, and some will even annihilate anyone who tries to expose them. The true nature of predators is eventually revealed when they turn on the very people who enabled them, so you don't have to worry about spending energy exposing the perpetrator, *unless* you have the proof, sense of personal safety, and incentive to do so. But first, make sure you have weighed the pros and cons of coming forward.

Some people find that the risk of retaliation and personal danger far outweighs the need to expose the perpetrator, while others believe that exposure can help prevent other victims from falling prey or even unite a group of past victims of the same predator to come forward together. It all depends on your specific circumstances, but in any case, your personal safety should always come first. Above all else, refocus on rebuilding your own name, healing, gaining social support, and meeting your personal goals.

JOURNAL REFLECTION: **Friend or Foe?**
Think about your current support network. Who's in it? Identify those who distance themselves or abandon you during a smear campaign—these people are showing their true colors. Also take note of who stands by your side—these are your true friends. If your entire support network is defunct, start identifying potential resources to build new ones. Research in-person support groups, social networking opportunities (like those on Meetup.com), counselors, and domestic violence centers in your area.

Triangulation

Bringing another person's threatening opinion, perspective, or presence into the dynamic of an interaction or relationship is known as *triangulation*. It is often used to validate the toxic person's abuse while invalidating the victim's reactions to abuse. Triangulation can take place across a variety of contexts and is used for the purposes of sabotage and bullying.

- It can come in the form of a love triangle that leaves you unhinged and insecure.

- Narcissistic parents triangulate by pitting two siblings against each other—they make unwarranted comparisons and manufacture sibling rivalry.

- A sociopathic ringleader of a social group can pit friends against one another by claiming that each person is gossiping about the other, when in reality, they are the one controlling each member of the group by spreading false information.

- In workplaces, toxic people can triangulate by spreading misinformation about a coworker to their boss to prevent them from getting a well-deserved promotion.

Triangulation in romantic relationships is used not only to maintain control but also to provoke jealousy. Malignant types in relationships love to triangulate their significant other with strangers, coworkers, ex-partners, friends, and even family members to evoke insecurity in you. They also use the opinions of others to validate their point of view and gaslight you about the abuse you're experiencing.

The narcissistic personality uses triangulation and harem-building to make themselves look like a highly sought after person with many options, whether that's the reality or not. In his book *The Art of Seduction*, Robert Greene encourages seducers to create "triangles" with friends, former lovers, and present suitors to stir rivalries and boost their value. This creates perceived competition so that the target becomes fixated on "winning" this "highly desirable" person's attention and affection. As Greene writes, "Few are drawn to the person whom others avoid and neglect; people gather around those who have already attracted interest. To draw your victims closer and make them hungry to possess you, you must create an aura of desirability—of being wanted and courted by many" (2004, 195).

Narcissists manufacture love triangles by constantly talking about their exes, people they've dated, or people who were apparently "obsessed" with them (of course, you'll later learn that these same people are the ones the narcissist terrorized). Excessive triangulation can be an early warning sign and a foreshadowing of future manipulation. For example, if you find that on a first date, someone talks at length about their former partners, those they find attractive, or those who find them attractive, *or* if they excessively flirt with others around them, consider this a major red flag and a blatant sign of disrespect.

Triangulation is a diversionary tactic meant to pull your attention away from abusive behavior and onto the false image of the person's desirability. A harem provides social proof of the narcissist's character. If you're the only one who has a "problem" with this person, *you* must be the problem—or so you assume. In reality, this only means that people agree to overlook the fact that the emperor has no clothes.

Manipulators employ triangulation to achieve many things— whether it be smear campaigns, gaslighting, or gaining narcissistic supply. It leaves you questioning yourself: If Danica did agree with Justin about how "crazy" you are, doesn't that mean you must be wrong? The truth is, narcissists love to "report back" gossip and lies that other people are supposedly saying about you when, in fact, *they* are the ones spreading the falsehoods.

Tips on Squaring Off Against Triangulation

To counter triangulation tactics, realize that whomever the narcissist is triangulating with is also being triangulated by *your* relationship with the narcissist. Everyone is essentially being played by this one person; there is no need to compete or work harder to capture the narcissist's approval or full attention. Reverse-triangulate the narcissist by gaining support from a third party who is not under the narcissist's influence, as well as by seeking your own validation and working on your self-esteem.

Self-love and nourishing your sense of irreplaceability can go a long way in protecting you from unnecessary comparisons and negative self-talk. Evaluate what is unique and lovable about you. What would people first notice about you? Learn to see yourself through fresh eyes and through the eyes of others who adore and cherish your strengths. Minimize comparing yourself to anyone else.

Break the triangle by removing yourself from the equation altogether. A healthy partner will strive to make you feel cherished and secure; an unhealthy one will manufacture and feed insecurities and position you as part of their harem. You never have to compete for a partner who is actually worthy of you. Take yourself out of the competition entirely, avoid comparisons, and honor your irreplaceability.

JOURNAL REFLECTION: **Uniquely You**

Write down ten "irreplaceable" qualities or assets you possess that contribute to your uniqueness. What is special about you and your life that someone meeting you for the first time would see? Look through the appreciative eyes of someone looking at you for the first time.

Preemptive Defense and Pathological Lying

Covert wolves in sheep's clothing are notorious for *virtue signaling*—publicly declaring sentiments that cast them in a good light and make others believe in their morality and character. When someone stresses the fact that they are a "nice guy" or "good person," asserts that you should trust them right away, or emphasizes their credibility without any provocation from you whatsoever, consider it a sign that you need to pay close attention to their character. According to internationally renowned security expert Gavin de Becker, author of *The Gift of Fear* (2010), this is a variation of what is known as an "unsolicited promise," something that predators will use to lower your defenses so they can prey on you.

Abusive people overstate their ability to be kind, loyal, honest, and compassionate. They claim they would "never lie to you" without first building a solid foundation of trust organically. This kind of preemptive defense is meant to protect them against your eventual, and inevitable, suspicions down the road. They can "perform" for you a high level of sympathy and empathy at the beginning of your relationship to dupe you, only to unveil their false mask and cruel intentions later on. When you see the mask slipping periodically during the devaluation phase of the abuse cycle, the true self is revealed to be terrifyingly calculating and contemptuous.

Genuinely nice or honest people rarely brag excessively about their positive qualities—they exude their warmth and consistency more than they talk about it; they know that their actions over time speak volumes more than mere words. They know that trust and respect is a two-way street that requires reciprocity, not repetition.

Narcissists, sociopaths, and psychopaths are natural pathological liars. As George Simon, PhD, asserts, "Manipulative malignant narcissists lie to keep one step ahead of you.... They neither want you to know who they really are nor what they're really up to. They seek only power, dominance, and control. And lying enables this. It gives them the position of advantage" (2018).

Lies can be explicit or they can be told with a significant amount of omission. As Donna, a survivor of narcissistic abuse, tells me, "The sneakiest way a covert narcissist abused me was obfuscation! Never giving all the facts so it wasn't ever a complete lie, but leaving me with a feeling of, *something is missing in the story*." Pathological deception like this is common among sociopathic leaders in the business world. For example, CEO Elizabeth Holmes defrauded investors out of billions of dollars for her blood-testing startup, Theranos, a technology that delivered none of what it promised. She was able to cultivate relationships with some of the world's wealthiest and most influential people using her charisma, leading some investors to hand over millions to a company that placed the health of others at stake. She was even said to be faking her voice in order to appear more dominant. Her prolific lies, along with the strength of her false persona, enabled her to get away with fraud for quite a long time.

Narcissists create these types of elaborate lies not only to commit financial fraud but also to engage in emotional con artistry. It's very common for them to live double lives and hide multiple affairs.

Tips for Dealing with Preemptive Defenses and Pathological Liars

Be wary of preemptive defenses. If someone declares early on that they would never lie to you, ask yourself why they feel the need to say that. Rather than taking their claims as truth, examine *why* a person may be emphasizing their good qualities. Is it because they think you don't trust them or because they know you shouldn't? Trust behavioral patterns more than empty words and see how someone's actions communicate who they are, not who they say they are.

Do not give your blind trust to anyone unless they have shown you the consistency of their character over time. Remain neutral at the beginning of any kind of relationship—whether it be a romantic relationship or a business venture. This will help you notice discrepancies and red flags. Be wary of anyone who "drip-feeds" you the truth, giving you only part of the truth while omitting important details. If you are especially vulnerable to gaslighting, I recommend keeping a journal to track any information that does not add up when meeting a new partner, friend, or employer. This will keep you grounded within your instincts and inner guidance.

Maintain a record, even if it has to be a secret record, of all the lies you suspect you've been told by someone and the evidence you've discovered that challenges them. Additionally, when confronting someone you suspect is a pathological liar, let them tell their version of events first by asking follow-up questions so you can observe whether or not they will tell the truth and what they let slip.

Remember, covert wolves in sheep's clothing reveal their true colors more readily when they think they're not being watched. If they are violent or aggressive, do not let them know you have contradictory information that would expose them. Instead, detach, make a safety plan, and cut ties as soon as possible. Taking an observer stance, instead of automatically accusing them, will give you more information about their character in the long run—mainly, whether they'd be willing to be transparent even if they didn't know you had proof of their lies. You are not responsible for filling the gap between the reality of this person and who they portray themselves to be.

JOURNAL REFLECTION: **Words, Actions, and Patterns**

Look at the toxic person's words, actions, and patterns. Write down a promise a toxic person has made you. Then write down the actions that contradicted these words. Next, write down the overarching patterns you've been noticing from this person in relation to this promise that appear to disprove the stated intentions. If you wish, you can also add a conclusion, as shown in this example:

Words: *He said he would never lie to me.*

Actions: *He had a secret girlfriend.*

Patterns: *A history of pathological lying, using charm and deceit to blindside me.*

Conclusion: *He is a pathological liar who preemptively tries to prove his trustworthiness. He cannot be trusted and does not belong in my life.*

Nonsensical Arguments and Conversational Diversions

Malignant narcissists weaponize a variety of conversational diversions to keep you off-balance and to engage in crazy-making. These include:

Ad hominem attacks and character assassination. When narcissists are unable to provide a logical rebuttal to your argument or perspective, they attack your character instead. They employ circular reasoning, insults, projection, and gaslighting to disorient you and get you off track should you ever disagree with them or challenge them in any way. They do this in order to discredit, confuse, and frustrate you, to distract you from the main problem and make you feel ashamed for being a human being with differing thoughts and feelings.

If you've ever spent even ten minutes arguing with a toxic narcissist, you've probably found yourself wondering how the argument even began at all. You simply disagreed with them about their absurd claim that the sky is red and now your entire childhood, family, friends, morality, career, and lifestyle choices have come under attack. That is because your disagreement picked at their false belief that they are omnipotent and omniscient, resulting in a threat to their overinflated sense of self and grandiose sense of superiority. Rather than addressing your feedback, they stage personal attacks on who you are as a person.

How to confront ad hominem attacks: The best response is, of course, no response, but if you do have to respond to a narcissist's attacks for whatever reason, do not give in to their diversion. Restate the facts and let them know that their personal attack is not relevant. If you can, end the conversation there. You don't owe grown adults a full education on how to be a decent person. Remember, toxic people don't argue with you; they essentially argue with themselves and you serve as the audience to their long, self-absorbed, draining monologues. They thrive off the drama, and they live for the chaos they manufacture. Each and every time you attempt to counter their absurd claims, you feed them narcissistic supply. Don't feed them—instead, supply yourself with the confirmation that their abusive behavior is the problem, not you. Cut the interaction short as soon as you anticipate it escalating and use your energy on self-care and self-protection instead.

Name-calling. As we know, narcissists blow out of proportion anything they perceive as a threat to their superiority. In their world, only they can ever be right, and anyone who dares to say otherwise creates an injury that results in narcissistic rage, which, as Mark Goulston, MD, asserts, does not result from low self-esteem, but from a high sense of entitlement and false sense of superiority. He writes, "Hell hath no fury or contempt as a narcissist you dare to disagree with, tell they're wrong or embarrass. There is a saying that when you're a hammer the world looks like a nail. When you're a narcissist, the world looks like it should approve, adore, agree and obey you. Anything less than that feels like an assault and because of that a narcissist feels justified in raging back at it" (2012).

The lowest of the low resort to name-calling when they can't think of a better way to manipulate your opinion or micromanage your emotions. They feel entitled to diminish and demean you by labeling you in destructive ways. Name-calling is a quick and easy way to degrade your intelligence, appearance, or behavior while invalidating your right to be a separate person with your own perspective.

Name-calling can also be used to criticize your beliefs, opinions, and insights. The wisdom you've gained from your life experiences, your well-researched perspective, or your informed opinion is depicted as "moronic" or "idiotic" in the hands of a malignant narcissist who feels threatened by it and cannot make a respectful, convincing rebuttal. Narcissists insult your intelligence to conceal their own ineptitude. Rather than target your argument, they target you as a person and seek to undermine your credibility and intelligence in any way they can.

How to handle name-calling: It's important to end any interaction that consists of name-calling and communicate that you won't tolerate it. It will only get worse from there. Don't internalize it: realize that this person is resorting to name-calling because they lack higher-level methods. You can follow these steps:

- If you find yourself becoming distressed due to the name-calling, use mindful breathing methods to calm down and refocus on how to best defend yourself in your specific circumstances.

- If name-calling happens during a discussion with a family member or an intimate partner, tell them firmly, "I won't tolerate being disrespected like that," and make a safe exit for the time being.

- If the name-calling takes place as a form of harassment or stalking by an ex-partner, be sure to document it in case you ever need it for legal action.

- If it occurs in a professional setting, analyze whether or not you can report the incident to a manager.

- If online, report the incident to the appropriate social media platform and block the person. Keep screenshots in case the person continues cyberstalking.

Sweeping generalizations. To avoid addressing the real issues at hand, narcissists make sweeping generalizations whenever we dare to call out their mistreatment. These include exaggerations about your hypersensitivity or all-encompassing statements such as, "You are *never* satisfied" and "You *always* overreact." This tactic can be especially powerful when used on HSPs, because it gaslights us into believing that it is our high sensitivity, rather than their abuse, that is the problem. While it's possible you *are* oversensitive at times, it is far more likely that the abuser is insensitive and cruel the majority of the time.

How to deal with sweeping generalizations: Toxic people wielding blanket statements do not represent the full richness or nuance of reality. They represent a distorted perspective based on their own self-absorbed agendas. Hold on to your truth and resist generalizations by realizing that they are, in fact, forms of illogical, black-and-white thinking. You can also point out, "You're generalizing. There have been many instances when this isn't true," depending on how receptive you think this person would be to feedback. However, the more toxic they are, the more likely you will get mired in a meaningless argument meant to throw you off-balance. The goal is not to become trapped in such an argument, but to stick to the original statement you're trying to get across and exit if this person resorts to personal attacks.

Misrepresenting your perspective to the point of absurdity. When you dare to disagree with a narcissist, your differing opinions, legitimate emotions, and lived experiences get translated into character flaws and "proof" of your irrationality and inability to think critically. This is also a common cognitive distortion known as "mind reading." Toxic people will claim they know what you're thinking and feeling by chronically jumping to conclusions based on their own triggers instead of evaluating the situation mindfully. These misrepresentations can stem from their own delusions and fallacies, but also from the need to deliberately unsettle you and detract from your perspective.

Narcissists tell tall tales that distort what you're actually saying so your opinions look absurd or downright heinous. Rather than acknowledging your emotions, the narcissist diverts from your experiences with outlandish accusations you didn't even make. For example, maybe you're unhappy with the way a toxic partner is speaking to you and you call them out. In response, your partner may put words in your mouth, saying, "Oh, so now *you're* perfect?" or "So I am an evil person, huh?" when you've done nothing but express your feelings. Or they may attack your character with something like, "So what you're saying is, I can't have an opinion. You're so controlling!" This enables them to invalidate your right to have thoughts and emotions about their inappropriate behavior, instilling a sense of guilt when you establish boundaries.

How to respond to misrepresentations: Set a firm boundary by repeatedly stating, "I never said that. Don't put words in my mouth." Then walk away should the person continue to accuse you of doing or saying something you didn't. Don't let this toxic person blame-shift and digress from their own abusive behavior or shame you for giving them any sort of realistic feedback. If you are dealing with someone you can't depart from (like in the workplace), it's helpful to succinctly repeat the facts of what you did do or say and excuse yourself.

Changing the subject to avoid accountability. This tactic is what I like to call the "What about *you?*" syndrome. It's a digression from the actual topic that redirects attention to a different issue altogether. Narcissists don't want you to hold them accountable for anything, so they will reroute discussions to circumvent consequences. Complaining about their neglectful parenting? They'll point out a child-rearing mistake you made ten years ago. Letting them know that their lies are unacceptable? They'll remark about that time you told a white lie to get out of a family event. This type of diversion has no limits in terms of time or subject content, and it often begins with a sentence like: "What about the time when *you* did this?"

How to avoid this diversion: Don't be derailed—if a toxic person pulls a switcheroo on you, exercise the broken-record method mentioned earlier by continuing to state the facts without giving in to the attempts to distract you from the bigger picture. Redirect *their* redirection by saying, "That's not what I am talking about. Let's stay focused on the real issue in the present moment."

Bait and feign innocence. Toxic individuals lure you into a false sense of security so they can showcase their cruelty in an even more appalling fashion. Provocative statements, hurtful "jokes," name-calling, stinging accusations, and unsupported generalizations are all common forms of baiting. A toxic partner may suddenly make a comment about how attractive a coworker is or inappropriately joke about wanting an affair. This is a lure to see if you will react. Baiting you into a mindless, chaotic argument can quickly escalate into a showdown when the person on the other end has no empathy or remorse for their tactless behavior.

A simple disagreement can bait you into responding politely initially, until it becomes clear that the person has a malicious motive of tearing you down. A covert put-down disguised as "just a joke" has a way of getting under your skin without being able to hold the offender accountable. These aggressive jabs cloaked as playful sparring allow verbal abusers to say the most horrific things while still maintaining an innocent, cool demeanor. Yet anytime you are outraged at an insensitive, harsh remark, you are usually accused of having no sense of humor. After all, it's just a joke, right? Wrong. It's a way to gaslight you into thinking their abuse is a joke—a way to divert you from their cruelty with your own perceived sensitivity.

By baiting you with an insulting comment posed as an innocuous one, they can then begin to play with your emotions. Remember, these types of predators are well aware of your vulnerabilities, your insecurities, the unsettling catchphrases that disrupt your confidence, and the disturbing topics that reenact and cause you to reexperience your original wounds—and they use this knowledge deviously to provoke you. After you've fallen for it hook, line, and sinker, they will sit back and innocently ask whether you're "okay" and talk about how they didn't "mean" to agitate you. This faux innocence catches you off guard and makes you believe they truly didn't intend to hurt you, until it happens so often that you can't deny the reality of their deliberate cruelty.

How to resist being baited: Notice when an off-color comment, a remark disguised as "playing devil's advocate," or a so-called joke disturbs you. There is usually a reason. It helps to realize *when* you're being baited so you can avoid engaging altogether. Your gut instinct can also tell you when you're being baited—if you continue to feel belittled even after clarification, this is a signal that you need to take some space to reevaluate the situation before choosing to respond.

Not everyone who disagrees with you will do so respectfully. You must remain mindful and vigilant of potential escalation. Rather than responding directly to the bait, you can say something neutral like, "Interesting," while excusing yourself. This offers little to no invitation to continue the conversation and avoids giving baiters the emotional reaction they're looking for.

You will, of course, have repeat offenders. Some toxic people will continue this behavior even when they don't get any emotional reaction. When this happens, it's important to stand up for yourself and make it clear that you won't tolerate this type of behavior by ending the interaction immediately and cutting off contact completely.

Calling out manipulative people on their covert put-downs may result in further gaslighting, but maintain your stance that their behavior is not okay. Embody your newfound strength by walking away from anyone who pokes and prods you for a reaction. As an HSP, you're never "too" sensitive to an insensitive person's provocations: you are right on point. Trust yourself.

How to Use CLEAR UP with a Narcissist

The CLEAR UP acronym presented in the previous chapter can be adapted specifically for dealing with narcissists and uncooperative individuals. You cannot effectively communicate with this type of person unless you take into account their lack of empathy and the reality of their disorder. But remember: if you fear you may be in any danger or your abuser has shown violent tendencies in the past, do not confront a narcissist directly.

Here is how to apply the CLEAR UP tool when you can't avoid communicating with a narcissist.

Context. When you frame the situation to a narcissist, refrain from overly emotional language and stick to the facts. It helps to avoid face-to-face confrontation and use email or text to document the interaction whenever possible. Narcissists thrive off the fuel of your emotional reactions and enjoy provoking people who are highly sensitive. Becoming less emotionally responsive to their tactics is part of a larger technique known as the "gray rock method," developed by a blogger named Skylar, a survivor of a psychopath. This is where you become like a boring gray rock to avoid a narcissist noticing you or wanting to actively manipulate you—almost like when an animal of prey plays dead to avoid the gaze of a predator.

Using less emotional language can work in your favor because the narcissist will not be getting as much of a rise from you and may therefore move on to "easier" prey they can provoke and manipulate. For example, if you are confronting someone who has lied to you about having another relationship, you might say something like, "I only have relationships with people who are honest with me. You told me prior to our date that you did not have a partner. Now I've found out you have a spouse." Using a calm, composed, even deadpan tone of voice while stating the facts (or maintaining neutral, short responses while communicating via text or email message) can help.

Lay down the law. When you express why the behavior you're experiencing is problematic, it's important to take the focus off of you and onto the potential consequences. One example: "If you do not stop contacting me, I will have to get law enforcement involved." Or you can opt for a more direct line of communication: "Stop harassing me." It's helpful to do this via text or email for documentation purposes.

Exercise boundaries. This can include stating directly what you desire, once and only once through electronic communication. For instance, in the scenario of the married person trying to reach out to you, you could write, "I do not get involved with married people. Please do not contact me again." If they persist in contacting you, you can block their number and any of their social media profiles through which they might communicate. If they use any anonymous accounts or multiple phone numbers to reach you, make sure you are documenting this information in case you ever need it for legal purposes.

Appreciation. Appreciation is not recommended with a narcissist in most situations because if you give an inch, they'll take a mile. However, you can appreciate your own needs; if you must negotiate in a situation where you cannot cut off contact (like at work), find a way to get some of your own needs met in the interaction. For example, if a coworker is asking you to take on the majority of the work on a project, tell them you will submit your half of the work after they've finished the first half. Make sure there is an "accountability" or "reciprocity" factor so that the person knows their needs will not be met unless yours are met first.

Repetition. Remember the facts and your objectives regardless of the numerous diversions a narcissist is likely to subject you to. If the cheater in the example above attempts to gaslight you by saying, "I don't have another partner. I have no idea what you're talking about. Could we meet up and discuss things?" you can respond with the broken-record technique and repeat: "I do not wish to see or hear from you again. I have evidence you have a partner, and I know the truth. Don't try to spin it; it won't work with me." Or you can say nothing at all, block their number, and simply *repeat to yourself* the reality you experienced. Anchoring yourself in this reality is just as, if not more, important. You don't need the narcissist's validation prior to exiting the exchange and taking care of yourself.

Unity. Narcissists usually don't agree to disagree peacefully, so never expect a fair negotiation with them. They will rage at you when you threaten their sense of entitlement. What's important, however, is unifying yourself with your goals, support network, outside resources, and empowering actions. Regardless of how *they* push back on your boundaries, you must continue to do what is best for you and hold them accountable. As you observe and gather information about the situation, document everything and trust that the narcissist will rarely keep their word. Documentation can also help if you choose to get an order of protection or need to take a case to court. Present a unified front within yourself by resisting the emotional manipulation they will inevitably use to get their way.

Power posing. Feigning confidence even when you're not feeling it is even more important when dealing with a narcissist, who is always looking for any signs of vulnerability. Again, avoid face-to-face confrontation if you can help it. If you can't, use the interaction to help boost your confidence. Take a safe third party along with you to mediate, to "witness," or to embolden you. If you are normally soft-spoken, take this opportunity to speak in a firm, neutral, yet unfaltering tone. Stand in a "power posture" if it'll help. Maintain eye contact.

JOURNAL REFLECTION: Plan Your Responses

Using the principles outlined in the examples above, map out your own CLEAR UP approach to deal with the narcissist in your life. What would you say? Who would you enlist to help serve as a witness? How would you build your confidence and anchor yourself in the reality of the abuse you experienced? How would you stay mindful?

Strategies to Exit

When you suspect you're dealing with a narcissistic individual, implementing the OFTEN acronym is a strategy you can use to remind you of your options to exit the situation:

Observe rather than accuse

Fade out

The handy excuse

Exit and make a safety plan

Notice rather than react

Observe rather than accuse. Narcissistic individuals tend to unmask themselves far more quickly when they think you're not aware of who they truly are. Direct confrontation of their narcissism will result in further manipulation and narcissistic rage, which can cause you to remain entrenched in the cycle of their abuse as they begin love bombing you again. If you suspect you're with a narcissist, the better route might be to mentally prepare how to leave while collecting more information about their character.

For example, if you're planning to divorce a narcissist, don't tell them until you have all your affairs in order. This might mean: consulting a divorce lawyer who specializes in high-conflict personalities, hiring a divorce financial planner to help you with your credit and finances, researching custody laws, getting a separate bank account, and finding a place to live.

Watch out for the red flags, and when you see them, self-validate without relying on the narcissist's counterexplanation (which is likely to be filled with pathological lying, gaslighting, projection, and half-truths). Their actions and patterns of behavior will tell you far more than their words ever will.

Fade out. A narcissist will rage when they feel slighted or rejected. Rather than outwardly rejecting them, you can do a slow "fade." Pretend that everything is as it was, but gradually give them less and less of your energy and time. Stick to one-word or neutral responses when in conversations with them. Incrementally pull out your investment so they get accustomed to not having you around. Narcissists cannot stand not having attention, so they will attempt to gain narcissistic supply elsewhere.

The handy excuse. When you fade out, it's important to have a "handy excuse"—something the narcissist deems plausible enough to explain your withdrawal rather than recognizing that you are actually ejecting their presence from your life. Pretend to be busy with a work project, emphasize how stressful your new coursework is, talk about a new venture that is taking up your time. If they react with additional rage, proceed to the next step.

Exit and make a safety plan. Eventually, you'll need to have a safety plan for your exit. Work with a counselor, your human resources department, or a domestic violence advocate to devise an escape strategy. Depending on the nature of your relationship with the narcissist and whether you're cohabiting with them, you may not have to make as many arrangements as you might think.

Notice rather than react. If you are forced to deal with a narcissist even after you've exited the relationship (such as in situations of co-parenting or family reunions), being emotionally in control is a must. As you know, narcissistic individuals enjoy provoking you. Notice their manipulation tactics, name them, and rather than giving them the reactions they are seeking, mindfully take a breath and refocus on your self-care. Know what they are trying to get from you, and you will achieve a sense of emotional freedom from their tactics.

CHAPTER FOUR

Toxic-Person Rehab
Breaking the Addiction and Going No Contact

Miranda couldn't understand why she wasn't able to get over Terence. She found herself constantly ruminating over the whirlwind romance they had, even though it had been months since the breakup. In the early periods of their relationship, he had showered her with lavish gifts, weekend getaways, and elaborate dates. He would call her day and night. Though there were times he seemed a bit cold and withdrawn, she was able to dismiss these red flags when he came back with the same fervent dedication to their relationship he had displayed in the beginning.

Later, he began putting her down and comparing her to other women, even lashing out in angry outbursts. He would disappear for days and ignore her, then come back as if nothing had happened. She would take him back, each and every time. Although she was finally the one to end things and cut all ties with him, her whole world was torn apart in the aftermath. The devastation was overwhelming. She craved to call him and reconcile, despite his mistreatment. She believed that if only they could "make things work," they could return to what they had in the beginning.

In the economics world, the *sunk cost fallacy* describes a phenomenon in which we continue to invest (time, money, or resources) in something because we have already paid a cost that cannot be unpaid. In the context of toxic relationships, the sunk cost fallacy applies to the time and energy we've spent investing in this particular person and the hope for a positive return, a payoff of some kind for the hefty emotional toll it's taken to maintain the relationship and the psychological debt we've incurred from enduring the trauma. We figure, "I've stayed this long, I can't just leave my investment now!" Like a gambler in a casino, rather than cutting our losses and realizing it would cost far less to leave now, we continue playing in hopes of that elusive "win."

Overcoming the fallacy requires accepting that while we can never regain the time we lost, we *can* reclaim our future and prevent any further cost to our well-being by leaving sooner rather than later. Freedom will be the payoff you are looking for. Yet freedom can be difficult to obtain when you still feel addicted to your narcissistic or otherwise toxic partner. In this chapter, you'll learn how to better manage your addiction to this relationship and reconnect to the reality of the situation.

No Contact Is a Gift to You

"No contact" creates a space for healing and reviving yourself, apart from the belittling influences of the toxic person. It is an opportunity for you to detach completely from them while moving forward with your life and pursuing your goals. It allows you to look at the relationship honestly from the realm of your own intuition, emotions, and thoughts, without gaslighting and abuse blurring your perspective.

Anyone who has treated you with disrespect does not deserve to be in your life. The rule of "no contact" helps you resist the temptation to invite them back into your life in any manner. Many survivors find it helpful to track their progress on a calendar or in a journal. You should celebrate and take note of your ability to maintain no contact, as it is both a challenging and a rewarding path to self-empowerment.

By establishing no contact, you are ultimately staging your own victory and exploring your strengths, talents, and new freedom with more ease. I invite you to take the first steps to successful recovery by challenging yourself to at least ninety days of no contact if you are undertaking this for the first time—that's the same amount of time needed for drug addicts to detox, and as you know, toxic love is akin to addiction. In this period of detoxification, you can start to heal in a protective space of self-care and self-love, enabling your mind and body to repair from the abuse.

Breaking the Biochemical Bonds

Remember when we talked about biochemical addiction in chapter 1? Now it's time to replace these bonds with toxic people with something constructive rather than destructive.

Dopamine

As you'll recall, dopamine is one of the guilty culprits in our infatuation with an inconsistent partner. This neurotransmitter is released more readily when rewards are intermittent and unpredictable, so the hot-and-cold behavior of narcissists actually serves our unhealthy addiction to them. Pleasure and pain combined make for a more "rewarding" experience for our brains than pleasure alone, and as a result, our brains pay more attention to these relationships. Break this toxic addiction by replacing it with these healthy alternatives.

Novelty

Take up new activities that will give you an adrenaline rush that has nothing to do with the toxic relationship. For HSPs who find activities like rock climbing, skydiving, or bungee jumping too alarming to their nervous system, do just one thing a day that scares you but that you know is beneficial for you. Brainstorm ways and activities to add spontaneity to your life to replace the high the narcissist used to give you. During my own journey of no contact, I used to look up different events on a daily basis to see what new adventure I could go on every day. This "intermittent schedule" of rewards allows dopamine in your brain to flow more readily, providing you space to explore novel hobbies and interests. Start actually doing the activities on your bucket list and make your anticipated schedule as unpredictable as your narcissist's hot-and-cold behavior was. This enables you to rebuild a more fulfilling life overall.

JOURNAL REFLECTION: **Bucket List**

Create a bucket list of things that push you to go beyond your comfort zone, adding an element of "healthy" fear without overstimulating yourself with respect to your sensitivity levels. On my journey, I went on a number of adventures that made life more interesting and exciting, from the super weird and silly to the rewarding and challenging—everything from riding a mechanical bull to going on my first-ever roller coaster. I also joined a new gym, got creative in an art therapy group, and tried hot yoga. Do things you've never done and do things you have done in a new way, whether it's just for fun or for a more targeted purpose—as long as it's brand new, your brain, body, and mind will thank you.

Productivity

Want to feed your reward system in more constructive ways? Create new reward circuits that keep you focused on your goals, dreams, and aspirations. Go after your passions and explore job opportunities that excite you. Get absorbed in a new hobby; volunteer to help those in need; jump-start a new creative project; enroll in a class or degree program that fascinates you and contributes to a mission you care about.

I've heard from many survivors who entered careers in counseling to help others like them; they found it especially empowering and fulfilling to give back due to their life experiences. While I was going no contact, I wrote books, got a new job, and met new people through Meetup.com. This gave back to my reward system in a way that was productive, not destructive. Doing this also rebuilds a better life with a new support system, adding a renewed sense of hopefulness that is essential to moving forward from a toxic relationship.

JOURNAL REFLECTION: **Goal Setting**

Write down at least ten goals, activities, or hobbies you could be pursuing right now to replace the time and energy you once spent on the narcissist.

Social Pleasure

HSPs need a social network that mirrors their own empathic natures. Go out with people who make you feel your best because they have positive, validating, and supportive attitudes. Pick friends who lift your spirits and hang out with them at your own pace. Honor the fact that social interactions can easily drain you by balancing solo time with just enough social pleasure to keep you energized rather than depleted.

Be selective about the company you keep. During recovery, stay away from or limit your interactions with people who trigger you. You know who I mean—the insensitive, invalidating types who only make you feel worse about yourself. Instead, socialize with the friends you always have a good time with, have deep and meaningful conversations with, the ones who make you laugh and who care for you deeply. *These* are the friends who can get that dopamine flowing again, but without the stress and trauma that toxic people bring.

JOURNAL REFLECTION: **Social Stimulation Limits**

How much social interaction is *too much* for you? When do you find yourself getting drained? For example, I feel drained if I go out two weekends in a row. I always need a weekend in between to do my own thing and recharge. Consider your social comfort level and stick to it.

Solitude

Just as social engagement is important, so is seeking pleasure solo. As an HSP, you process things very deeply. You have the gifts of introspection, imagination, and creativity. Use these as you take time and space to recharge your mental batteries. Spending time alone gets you accustomed to the peace and joy that is available without a toxic person in your life. Enjoyable solo activities can include dining out, going to a spa, soaking in a bubble bath with scented oils and candles, getting a massage, buying yourself a new outfit, going on a trip to a different city or even country you've always wanted to explore—the possibilities are endless. This will make you more independent and less people-pleasing because the more you relish solo experiences, the less likely you are to tolerate toxic people just for the sake of having company.

JOURNAL REFLECTION: **Solo Breaks**

What are three small things you can enjoy on your own this week (examples: go for a bike ride, read at the park, go for a walk by the river)?

Self-Care Pro-Tip. To add an adrenaline rush, incorporate the element of surprise to these solo activities whenever possible by introducing something "new"—a food you haven't tried, a place you haven't visited, or a game you've never played. Travel somewhere new for at least a weekend, even if it's just to a bed-and-breakfast in a different town or state.

Oxytocin

As you learned in chapter 1, oxytocin is that pesky love hormone that causes us to trust toxic people, even when they're not trustworthy. It is released during physical intimacy. Replace the oxytocin bond with the narcissist with any of the following options.

Withdrawal from Contact

Going "no contact" or "low contact" (the minimum contact necessary in situations that require ongoing ties, like co-parenting or workplace interactions) is essential to start to wean off of the effects of the oxytocin bond, although of course it will come with cravings to reconnect with the narcissistic partner. Rather than giving in to this temptation, supplant that craving with healthier connections.

Pet Therapy

Oxytocin isn't just released when you snuggle with loved ones; you can also produce oxytocin by cuddling a cute animal. Research shows that cuddling with a dog actually increases the oxytocin levels of both the dog and its owner while lowering cortisol levels in humans (Odendaal and Meintjes 2003). If you don't already have a pet, dog-sit for a friend, visit a pet store or an animal shelter, or, if you can, adopt a pet.

Physical Touch

Oxytocin can be released through physical touch with anyone we have a positive relationship with (Handlin, Petersson, and Uvnäs-Moberg 2015). Make it a regular habit to give hugs to the people you care about. Once you've ended the relationship with your narcissistic partner, you can even engage in safe touch with someone you're attracted to, as long as you're comfortable doing so, see them only as a casual partner, and are able to distinguish between physical contact and emotional connection. During this time of recovery, attempting to forge a long-term relationship is discouraged unless you've already healed considerably.

Casual Flirting

Keep it simple: interact with, talk to, or go on a casual date with someone with no strings attached—but only if you can keep your expectations and investment very low. Be mindful that engaging in sexual activity potentially bonds you to this person and can be triggering and retraumatizing, so act accordingly depending on what you feel you can handle. We're not trying to create another bond with a potentially toxic partner here—we're just opening up the opportunity for flirtation and social interaction.

This technique won't work for those who aren't able to separate physical affection from something more serious. But for others, going on a simple date or flirting with someone new can provide a pleasurable distraction and help the survivor get back on the path of feeling like a lovable, desirable human being. It will also remind you that you have options for close contact and intimacy with people other than the narcissist.

Compassion and Community Outreach

Oxytocin can increase compassion and pro-social behavior in those suffering from the symptoms of post-traumatic stress disorder (PTSD) (Palgi, Klein, and Shamay-Tsoory 2016). Given this connection between oxytocin and compassion, it might help to support a friend, donate to a cause, volunteer for a worthy mission, or lend a listening ear to someone. Not only will you help someone, but it'll make you feel better as well. It's a win-win situation that benefits everyone.

It's also important to show self-compassion, as research indicates that this heightens oxytocin levels and lowers cortisol. According to self-compassion expert Kristin Neff (2011), crossing your arms over your chest and placing your hands over your heart can release oxytocin. You can give yourself a hug like this whenever you need it. Loving-kindness meditations can also help increase compassion toward yourself and others, decreasing cortisol in the body (Rockliff et al. 2008).

Cortisol

Cortisol is a hormone we want *less* of, not more of. Author and coach Christopher Bergland (2013) suggests numerous ways to counteract its effects, including physical activity, mindfulness, meditation, laughter, music, and social connectivity. As you're healing, follow up on some of these suggestions to decrease your cortisol levels:

- Attend a weekly yoga flow class or join a daily class online

- Incorporate a ten-minute breathing meditation into your morning routine every single day

- Watch more comedy shows and movies to tickle your funny bone; laughter lowers cortisol levels and positively feeds your reward system

- Smile whenever you can—it releases endorphins that increase relaxation

- Plan a night out with your most supportive friends

- Join a forum or support group for abuse survivors

- Listen to music that expresses the different stages of grief and anger you are experiencing

- Volunteer at a community center

- Do loving-kindness meditations and affirmations to increase self-compassion

Relaxing and self-soothing are key to detaching from the narcissist in your life. They help you step back and overcome your cravings to reconnect with your narcissistic partner.

Serotonin

This powerful hormone can cause ruminative addiction to your ex-partner when levels are low; it affects impulsivity, ability to act on plans, emotions, memory, weight, sleep, and self-esteem. To increase serotonin, try these natural boosters, some suggested by researcher Alex Korb (2011):

- **Sunlight:** Exposure to sunlight increases serotonin levels. Take morning and afternoon walks whenever it is sunny to get your daily dose.

- **B-vitamins:** Low levels of serotonin can cause depression. B-vitamins are essential for the creation of both dopamine and serotonin, and research notes a link between inadequate amounts of vitamins like B_6 and B_{12} and depression (Mikkelsen,

Stojanovska, and Apostolopoulos 2016). Consult with your doctor about taking B-vitamin supplements to potentially lower the risk of depression.

- **Massage:** Research shows that massage therapy can help lower cortisol levels and boost serotonin and dopamine levels, alleviating stress (Field et al. 2005).

- **Happy memories:** Recalling happy memories can increase serotonin production in the anterior cingulate cortex, a part of the brain that controls attention. Look through old photo albums, old journals, and home movies if you need help visualizing happy memories. Doing so creates a dual effect: we increase serotonin while simultaneously preventing ourselves from ruminating over unhappy events. Take care not to recall or romanticize happier times with your abusive ex-partner; instead, make a gratitude list of memories unrelated to your abuser.

Therapy

An effective way to break unhealthy bonds is to talk to a mental health professional experienced in toxic relationships, addiction, and trauma bonding. Someone who is well versed and validating in these topics can help you uncover wounds beneath the surface you may not be aware of. I'll talk more about different types of therapy in the last chapter.

Medications

There are medications that can help if you are struggling with severe, crippling anxiety or depression, such as selective serotonin reuptake inhibitors, or SSRIs. However, they are beyond the scope of this book to discuss. Please always consult your psychiatrist or mental health professional regarding the best medication for you to take. Do not ever "replace" medication you are taking with any of the recuperative tools presented here, as they are meant as a supplement to your self-care regimen, not a substitute for therapy.

Exercise

This is a powerful mood booster because it can target numerous biochemicals all at once, resulting in a surge of neurotransmitters like norepinephrine, dopamine, and serotonin. Exercise can lower cortisol levels as well. Thankfully, there are plenty of creative ways to exercise. I've done everything from taking hip-hop dance classes to cardio kickboxing, but my favorite exercise of choice remains running. I highly encourage you to get a gym membership and join your local yoga center if you haven't already. Whether you're currently in an abusive relationship, planning to leave, or have already started the journey to cutting off contact, any form of exercise—whether it be hiking, belly dancing, strength training, Pilates, martial arts, biking, or Zumba—will act as a natural antidepressant and help you cope with your emotions more effectively at every stage of recovery.

Because we can become biochemically and traumatically bonded to toxic people in intimate relationships, it becomes more difficult for us to leave. When it comes to adverse relationships, our brains tend to work *against us* rather than for us, which is why we have to work even harder to cut ties and remember that our preoccupation with this person has more to do with the traumas of the relationship than the merits of the person. If we can better understand the addictive nature of these toxic relationships without blaming ourselves or justifying staying, then we can use this understanding to create healthier addictions and detach from toxic people.

Tips for Going No Contact or Low Contact

The ending of an unhealthy relationship can leave us reeling and feeling unable to cope. Although we know logically that we don't deserve abuse, we can be tempted to stray from this conviction when our emotions get ahold of us. Trauma bonds keep us tethered to the abuser, along with other factors such as codependency, low self-esteem, and low self-worth, which may have been instilled in us from the abusive relationship or kept us in the relationship in the first place. Here are some tips for sustaining low to no contact.

Have a schedule filled with fulfilling, feel-good activities. If no contact is a struggle for you, establish a weekly schedule filled with pleasurable, distracting activities, such as spending time with friends, going to a comedy show, getting a massage, taking long walks, and reading helpful books.

Mindfully manage addiction cravings. Remember that we are literally "addicted" to the narcissist via biochemical bonds created by love bombing, devaluation, and trauma. Take care of your physical and mental well-being by exercising daily, establishing a regular sleep schedule to keep your circadian rhythms in balance, doing yoga to strengthen your body and relieve stress, and engaging in a daily meditation practice of your choice. Studies show that mindfulness reduces our cravings (Bowen et al. 2009; Westbrook et al. 2011). You may also experiment with other alternative healing methods discussed further in the final chapter, such as acupuncture and aromatherapy.

Practice radical acceptance. Develop a healthier relationship with your cravings to break the no contact rule by practicing *radical acceptance*—wholly accepting life as it is in the present moment and not resisting what you cannot control. Remember that relapse may be an inevitable part of the addiction cycle. Forgive yourself if you do fall off the wagon by reestablishing contact at any point, but then get back on it with self-compassion and self-forgiveness. Track your urges in your journal. Make sure that before you act on any urge, you give yourself at least an hour to collect yourself. This will get easier once you realize that contacting your toxic ex-partner, friend, or family member often bears no rewards, only painful learning experiences.

Follow the delay rule whenever possible. When you have a compulsion for self-sabotage or are tempted to act on a harmful impulse (such as breaking no contact by reaching out to your abuser), delay action. Wait at least a day to see how you feel and assess whether you want to act on this craving. Keep delaying until the urge passes. Reach out for support during this time; talking with a trusted friend or counselor can help support you and hold you socially accountable for protecting yourself from toxic people.

EXERCISE: Craving Management

Whenever a craving to break no contact arises, visualize it as the ebb and flow of a wave, coming and going. It will pass. If you do have a relapse, radically (nonjudgmentally) accept your misstep and get back on track as soon as possible. Relapse can happen in addiction, but recovery will come with continued commitment.

Seek supportive communities. Social accountability is vital when it comes to changing unhealthy behavior. Look up online forums or communities related to being an HSP or to recovery from unhealthy and toxic relationships. Joining such encouraging forums provides you with a solid support network as you work to remain no contact and, as an added bonus, is an opportunity to support others like you who are also struggling. Furthermore, it validates the experiences you went through with peer support.

EXERCISE: Community Support

Research one virtual or real-life community you can join this week.

Take the time to grieve. You will likely experience grief during this time of withdrawal from the toxic person in your life. Know that this is normal and that grieving is often cyclical. There is no time limit. It's a fact: the more you resist negative thoughts and emotions, the more they'll persist. It is the emotional processing of your traumas that helps in healing, not avoidance. So learn how to accept both your emotions and the grieving process as inevitable parts of the healing journey. I recommend trying the grieving exercises in the book *Getting Past Your Breakup*, written by certified grief counselor Susan Elliot (2009).

JOURNAL REFLECTION: Confront an Emotion

What is one emotion you've been trying to avoid? Write down your thoughts and feelings related to this emotion.

Establish the parameters of low contact. If you are going low contact rather than no contact with an abuser due to a situation like co-parenting, business obligations, or because it's a parent you're not ready to cut ties with, consider what forms of contact you *can* tolerate. Do you want to allow phone calls or only texts? Will you visit for holidays, or will you have no in-person contact except for emergencies? These are questions to consider as you limit the ways the toxic person can reach you.

JOURNAL REFLECTION: Low-Contact Boundary-Setting

What is one boundary you can set right now to make low contact easier for you? For instance, can you block the toxic person from calling you and use a Google Voice number exclusively for texting? This could give you a break from their incessant communication and allow you to read what they have to say only when you're ready, if at all.

CHAPTER FIVE

Boundaries
Electric Fences That Ward Off Predators

In order to continually protect ourselves from toxic people and unhealthy situations, we need to better understand how to exercise boundaries as a natural instinct, rather than as a last-ditch effort at self-protection. It is better to have these boundaries in place *before* you invest in unhealthy relationships—before toxic predators are able to infiltrate your life and before they do great damage. Boundaries are our physical, emotional, sexual, and psychological "limits"—and HSPs must find ways to implement them even more fiercely, as we are prone to being taken advantage of.

Boundaries are figurative fences drawn to protect us from toxic individuals who violate our basic rights, interfere with our core values, and disrupt our personal sense of safety. When you have a clearer understanding of what your boundaries, rights, and deal-breakers are, you become more consistent when implementing healthy boundaries with others, warding them off before they are able to enter your head-space in the first place.

This acronym will remind you of what boundaries are and how we can maintain them:

Believe in your own worth

Own your agency

Understand your core values

Name your nonnegotiables

Deal-breakers—know them

Assert without apologies

Reinforce and repeat if challenged

Implement practically and safely

Exit when not respected

Save yourself and prioritize your self-care

Believe in your own worth. First, build confidence in yourself and trust that you are *worthy* of establishing your boundaries. In order to have boundaries, you must also have a solid sense of believing that you are on some level deserving of self-protection and getting your needs met. Use the diverse healing modalities discussed at the end of this book to "reprogram" your negative self-talk so that a belief in your worthiness becomes your default way of thinking and behaving.

When you believe you are worthy of being treated well and take steps to align your subconscious with that belief, miracles can and will occur. You will operate more assertively with others because your automatic programming is no longer saying, "I am not good enough" or "I am hypersensitive, don't mind me, let me bite my tongue and quietly shrink," but rather, "I *am* good enough. I *am* worthy. I deserve to be respected. I deserve to get my needs met too. I *am* sensitive, and that's a beautiful thing."

Own your agency. Many HSPs have interpersonal patterns of helplessness and powerlessness. As an HSP, you might believe that things will never change or that you can never stand up for yourself due to your fear of confrontation. Conflict can feel debilitating to an HSP because it overwhelms the nervous system and sends us straight into fight, flight, freeze, or fawn (people-pleasing) mode, in which we are likely to respond to manipulators in maladaptive ways. These amygdala hijackings override our rational decision making as we regress back into past wounds and fears, reacting in ways that serve the manipulator or put our safety at risk (Walker 2013; van der Kolk 2014).

Owning our agency means examining various options for how to cope with a situation effectively. This requires skillfully assessing the pros and cons of a situation, mindfully addressing our discomfort so we act out of confidence, exploring what we can control and change, and addressing the reality of a situation instead of turning to wishful thinking or our learned sense of helplessness.

Understand your core values. Reacquaint yourself with your foundational values and basic rights. Remind yourself on a daily basis that you have a right to protect yourself from abuse, exploitation, and mistreatment. You have a right to respectfully protest the toxic behavior of others and to detach from them. You have a right to safe, healthy, respectful communication with others. You have a right to take a break. You have a right to privacy. You have a right to not be an emotional punching bag or emotional sponge for toxic people. You have a right to dislike someone or their behavior.

Know your core values, learn the needs behind these values, and set your boundaries based on how you can honor those needs. For example, if you value success, then you might need a partner who cheerleads you rather than puts you down on your career path. You might honor that core value and need by keeping people out of your life who do not support your career or ambition.

You can assess your core values by looking at experiences throughout your life that have caused you to come into conflict with your internal guidance or moral radar. Perhaps you struggled recently in a situation where someone asked you to lie for them. A core value for you might thus be honesty. You believe in being honest, even when it is difficult. Your core values may include integrity and conscientiousness. You believe in doing the right thing over instant gratification, even when it requires a sacrifice on your part. Knowing your core values will help you recognize the type of people who will be compatible with you long-term.

Name your nonnegotiables. Depending on the type of toxic person you're dealing with, you will want to name your nonnegotiables, at the very least to *yourself* so you know them. Sometimes communicating a nonnegotiable looks like having a conversation with a garden-variety boundary-trespasser who is receptive to understanding your boundaries. However, if you're dealing with a narcissist who will use your nonnegotiables against you by provoking you deliberately, it's far better to have a solid understanding of what you will and won't tolerate, then step back without explanation or justification when you see red-flag behavior.

Your nonnegotiables may vary slightly from context to context, but they protect your basic rights as a human being worthy of respect and compassion. Nonnegotiables could include things like, "Nobody gets to raise their voice at me" or "No one gets to speak condescendingly to me." As HSPs, we're often told we're too sensitive to how people treat us. Yet our discomfort is legitimate and valid and should be expressed in healthy and assertive ways. With a narcissist who chronically mistreats you, these boundaries can be implemented immediately without justification or explanation as you withdraw from the interaction altogether. With a garden-variety boundary-trespasser who is receptive to feedback, they can be called out assertively as we step back and observe future behavior.

Deal-breakers—know them. Personal deal-breakers are the nonnegotiables that are not necessarily universal to everyone. They have more to do with our unique comfort levels. For example, you may have a personal deal-breaker in the dating world in the form of only wanting to date someone who is vegan. Or maybe a personal deal-breaker is that you don't wish to date anyone who doesn't foresee having children in the future. Someone else might have a personal deal-breaker of only wanting to date nonsmokers. Your personal deal-breakers don't have to be "right" or "wrong" in any moral sense. They are there to protect you, your individuality, and your investment. Personal deal-breakers allow you to establish healthy relationships and friendships with people who are most compatible with you in your core values and goals.

Assert without apologies. As HSPs, we've been conditioned to apologize for our thoughts, emotions, and reactions. It's important to assert ourselves without feeling guilty for standing up for our rights. An apology undercuts our right to protest unfair or unjust behavior and undermines our stance. You can assert yourself in a calm, rational manner without having to downplay the power of your assertion. Only apologize when you have done something wrong. If you have a habit of saying "I'm sorry" even when referencing less-than-ideal circumstances rather than actual blunders, get into the habit of asking yourself daily, "Does this require an apology?" If not, learn to replace "I'm sorry" with "That's unfortunate." You can express disappointment that the circumstances are what they are, but if you are not personally responsible for them, you do not owe anyone an apology.

Reinforce and repeat if challenged. With any boundary, there's a possibility that it will be challenged at the onset, especially if we're dealing with a toxic person. That's when we'll have to exercise the broken-record technique discussed previously and steadily keep implementing the boundary regardless of how a toxic person tries to convince us otherwise. As we also learned earlier, repeating ourselves will work differently with different types of people. With malignant narcissists, repetition is not always necessary because they're unwilling to self-reflect. It's far better to repeat yourself through action, by enacting your boundaries and presenting consequences consistently (in the form of your absence or legal consequences if warranted).

Implement practically and safely. It's not enough to know what our boundaries are; we actually have to put them to use. Set your boundaries in place with an eye on what is safest and most practical for you. It takes practice, trial and error, to know what works best for you in certain situations and with specific people. If you're already heavily invested in a relationship or friendship with someone who is *not* a malignant narcissist, it is usually best to assert your boundary so they are aware of it and what you will do if it is trespassed. For example, you might set a boundary with a flaky friend by telling her that if she doesn't confirm plans by a certain time, you will ask someone else to go with you.

However, there are other situations in which immediate implementation of a boundary is appropriate and the boundary should have been *implicitly understood*. For example, if your boundary is that you will not allow anyone to speak to you in a condescending manner, the next time you have a first date with someone who shows contempt, you might immediately excuse yourself and choose not to see that person again. Although you have the option of explaining your departure in this situation if you feel it's worth doing so, it's not necessary so early on with a stranger when no investment has yet been made.

In fact, there will be certain situations where it's best to practice your boundaries without openly talking about them. Like when? When you don't know a person yet and don't know what they're capable of. Take the above example: your date has already trespassed one of your boundaries before you even had a chance to form a connection to them. If this person can't even grasp the basic rules of human decency and respect in the very beginning of a relationship—in the "honeymoon phase," when things are supposed to be ideal and positive—things will only get worse from there, so there's no point at all in ongoing communication with them. It is not your responsibility to fix or change them. This person is an adult, responsible for their own behavior. It's your duty to *yourself* to make a speedy exit when you experience toxicity like this.

Malignant narcissists test your boundaries early on. Remember that the word "no" is a complete sentence, not an invitation for a negotiation. If someone tries to persistently negotiate your "no," that speaks volumes about how much they are willing to infringe upon your boundaries to meet their own needs.

Exit when not respected. When our boundaries are consistently disrespected or when in the presence of red flags, it's important to exit safely from the situation. This could look like brainstorming ways to leave a toxic workplace while searching for another job. It could look like making a safety plan to leave your abuser with the help of a therapist and with the resources of a domestic violence shelter. Be prepared to walk away if someone refuses to respect your boundaries and rights. You don't have to live in the cesspool of someone else's dysfunction.

Save yourself and prioritize your self-care. Many HSPs, especially those who experienced childhood abuse or emotional neglect, often disregard their own needs in order to cater to the desires of others. They develop a "savior complex" whereby they're driven to come to the rescue of others or routinely play the role of caretaker. This is especially true if they were raised by a parent who struggled with addiction or mental illness.

Due to our high sensitivity and empathy, HSPs are devoted "saviors" of others, but we forget to save ourselves. This mentality interferes with our ability to establish healthy boundaries. We believe we are responsible for "fixing" people and end up investing in toxic relationships with no positive return. The only people who benefit from these one-sided affairs are the ones we endlessly give to. It's important to prioritize your own self-care when you're dealing with a toxic person. You are not anyone's personal therapist (unless you actually *are* a therapist—in which case, you'll still need professional boundaries with your clients). This is not about being selfish. In fact, when you put your welfare first, you can help others with more stamina and effectiveness than would otherwise be available if you'd completely exhausted your resources.

The BOUNDARIES acronym presents general guidelines for dealing with all types of toxic people, which means you'll have to adapt the steps accordingly depending on whether you're dealing with someone benign or malignant. In either case, the goal is to shift from a disempowered HSP to an empowered one (see a helpful chart distinguishing between the two at http://www.newharbinger.com/45304).

JOURNAL REFLECTION: **Envisioning Enforcing Boundaries**

Think about a time when you've had a boundary violated in the past. How did it make you feel? What can you do the next time a boundary is violated like that?

Example: *My boundary was disrespected when my toxic friend continued to call me names as a "joke." Even though I told her I felt uncomfortable when she did that, she continued name-calling. In the future, the next time someone calls me a name or disrespects me, I will give them one chance to stop. If they don't, I will either detach from the friendship or cut all contact with them.*

Letter from an HSP to a Toxic Person

One of the most popular tools I've published has resonated with empathic people all over the world. It is a letter from us HSPs to the toxic people of the world. When in doubt, refer to this letter and use it as you wish to help you remember why boundaries are important and why they are so necessary for your self-care.

> *While I love to help others, I am not responsible for fixing your life or catering to your toxicity. I am not responsible for managing your triggers, walking on eggshells, or telling you what you want to hear in order to keep the peace. I am not your emotional punching bag nor am I your emotional sponge. I do not exist for your pleasure or as a site for your projected pain. My responsibility is to myself—to be my own person and stay true to myself—to heal my own wounds, manage my own triggers, and engage in self-care so I can give to others authentically without depleting myself in the process. My responsibility is to maintain healthy boundaries, especially with those who are unhealthy.*

JOURNAL REFLECTION: **Boundary-Setting Rights**

Complete the following two sentences with what you want to remind yourself.

I have a right to ...

Examples:

- I have a right to say "no."

- I have a right to change my mind.

- I have a right to be treated with respect.

- I have a right to reject unsolicited feedback, unsolicited advice, pressure, or personal attacks.

- I have a right to exit toxic and abusive relationships.

- I have a right to my beliefs, preferences, and opinions, even if others disagree.

It's okay for me to protect myself by ...

Examples:

- It's okay for me to protect myself by canceling a commitment.

- It's okay for me to protect myself by having alone time to unwind and recharge.

- It's okay for me to protect myself by cutting off toxic friendships.

- It's okay for me to protect myself by asking for help when I am overwhelmed.

- It's okay for me to protect myself by accepting compliments and rejecting insults.

- It's okay for me to protect myself by trusting myself and my instincts.

NOTE: A fuller version of this exercise can be found at http://www .newharbinger.com/45304.

Three Red Flags

When assessing the compatibility or potential toxicity of a partner, friend, coworker, boss, or family member, see what they focus on long-term in the following scenarios.

1. When you talk about your big dreams or accomplishments, do they provide consistent encouragement and support, or do they focus on what is lacking and subject you to covert put-downs and fearmongering comments?

2. When you bring up struggles you are going through, do they focus on emotionally validating you and being there for you, or do they shift the attention back to themselves or shame or judge you, making you feel even worse than you did before?

3. When you celebrate a milestone, do they make the special occasion even better by sharing in your joy, or do they minimize, deflate, or even sabotage your happiness?

Three Violations and You're Out

When in doubt about whether to continue engaging with someone, follow the "three violation rule," inspired by Martha Stout's book *The Sociopath Next Door* (2005). When a person mistreats you once, address it, then pull back from them a bit to observe whether they'll do it again. If they do it a second time, start withdrawing your investment in the relationship because they're showing you that they don't have an interest in respecting your boundaries. If they do it a third time, exit completely.

Following this rule early on when meeting new people can save you a lifetime worth of pain and can prevent you from investing in the wrong people long-term. This is also a good way to avoid wolves in sheep's clothing who disguise their predatory nature—you can set boundaries more swiftly and effectively when you recognize red flags early on.

EXERCISE: **Basic Self-Care Checklist**

Having boundaries with *yourself* is important too. We need personal boundaries in terms of how we speak to ourselves, how we take care of ourselves, and the access we give ourselves to basic self-care. Don't forget the basics—they make the difference between a good day and a stressful one. Make photocopies of the following checklist or re-create it on your computer or smartphone so you can complete it daily to attend to your own fundamental needs:

☐ Have I eaten today?

☐ Have I taken a shower?

☐ Have I taken a walk outside for fresh air and sunlight?

☐ Have I gently challenged my negative self-talk?

☐ Have I engaged in some form of exercise?

☐ Have I decluttered a bit, organized an area, or otherwise improved my surroundings?

☐ Have I listed five things I'm grateful for?

☐ Have I meditated?

☐ Have I showed myself compassion?

☐ Have I validated my emotions?

CHAPTER SIX

Prepare Your Arsenal
Self-Care Strategies and Reframing Skills for Everyday Life

HSPs operate in emotional ways of thinking and responding, so reframing skills can help us restructure harmful beliefs that contribute to people-pleasing habits and self-sabotaging thoughts that dampen assertiveness. The ability to reframe a situation to manage conflict and set boundaries is crucial to our well-being.

As HSPs, we actually do have great instincts about the toxic people we encounter. We pick up on the emotional states of others rapidly, notice subtleties in our environment, and make accurate, in-depth assessments about the situation at hand. The problem is, HSPs second-guess themselves more than other people and engage in self-blame because we've been chronically told we're "too" sensitive. It's *so* important not to blame ourselves for the toxic actions of others, especially abusive actions—that only gaslights us into staying in unhealthy situations instead of finding ways to protect ourselves. When we don't challenge beliefs that inadvertently enable manipulative people, we're less able to exit toxic situations.

Many HSPs go into counseling or coaching with the hope that their experiences will be validated, their sensitivity honored, and their pain heard. Unfortunately, that doesn't always happen when certain reframing skills that are taught are used maladaptively to further invalidate the HSP's perception of a situation. That's why here, in this chapter, we will be tailoring some therapeutic strategies to guide HSPs toward self-trust, boundary-setting, healthy assertiveness, and conflict management. You can still reframe harmful beliefs without invalidating your experiences, emotions, and intuition.

Reframing is often used to address cognitive distortions that create a "faulty" outlook on a situation. These distorted ways of thinking seem rational and accurate, but they in fact keep us trapped in negativity—whether that web of negativity is spun by ourselves or by a toxic person. As you review some of the common cognitive distortions HSPs engage in, see if you recognize them from your own life.

Black-and-White Thinking

Black-and-white thinking causes us to identify something as "all good" or "all bad" without taking into account the complexity or nuances of a situation. As HSPs, we view *ourselves* in this way. We view our manipulators as "all good" because of their superficial, glib charm and false mask, missing their red-flag behaviors. We see ourselves as "too sensitive" and "reactive" and our manipulators as "logical" and "composed" when, in fact, there is more dimension to our reactions and interactions than we realize. Due to our intuitive abilities, we are able to pick up on the subtleties of contexts and people. We need to acknowledge that while there can be situations in which we are overly reactive, most of the time, we are actually correct in our discernment of a toxic person's behaviors and intentions.

Catastrophizing

This distortion causes us to magnify situations and their perceived negative outcomes. HSPs tend to catastrophize the consequences of standing up for themselves. Our anxiety around conflict leads us to fear that if we don't please others, we'll be "doomed" to be alone forever. We tell ourselves things like, "I can't stand up to her—she's my boss! I'll be so humiliated if she disagrees! I'll die!" or "I can't say no to him, he'll be displeased, and I don't know when I'll ever get this opportunity again!" We also fear the ending of intimate relationships, so we bend over backward and abandon our boundaries to maintain the relationship, no matter how harmful it is.

Personalization

Personalization involves attributing someone else's choices, preferences, or external events to yourself. You may personalize rejection, for example, as an indication of your self-worth or attractiveness, dismissing the evidence that proves you're a desirable human being. You may feel you "caused" someone to react in a toxic way or take on responsibility for defusing someone's emotions. This is likely if you're dealing with a manipulative individual who blames you for *their* abusive actions or claims you "provoked" them. HSPs inhabit the role of "emotional caretakers" and forget to hold others accountable for their actions and reactions.

Mind Reading

In this cognitive distortion, you presume to know what another person is feeling and thinking. HSPs often project their own sense of morality and conscience onto toxic people who are drastically different in how they think and feel. A good way to "mind read" more accurately is to observe a toxic person's behavior and patterns, not their words or who you wish they were. Their behavior speaks volumes. Are they persistent in trying to get you to change your mind even when you say no? Do they harass and stalk you, becoming easily enraged? Do they engage in hot-and-cold behavior while claiming you're their first priority? If there is a huge discrepancy between their charming facade of goodwill and their harmful actions, this is a good indication that they are not who they claim they are.

How to Reframe Your Distortions About Self

Here's a straightforward process that challenges cognitive distortions about yourself, moving them into a positive sphere in four, easy-to-follow steps:

1. Identify a distortion to work on.

2. Write down evidence both for and against this distortion, including any identified origins for this belief (such as beliefs your parents passed down to you, the effects of childhood experiences or past relationships).

3. Reframe the distortion into one that provides a more balanced point of view.

4. Identify how to shift your behavior in line with this more balanced perspective, in a way that positively affects you.

Although I've come across myriad distorted thought patterns among HSPs in my work, I've chosen three of the most common ones to illustrate how reframing looks in real life. But keep in mind that these are just examples—yours might be completely different, so you'll want to tailor the content to your own experiences and needs.

Sample Distortion #1: I Can't Trust Myself

Evidence supporting this statement might be: As a child, I was gaslighted into believing I could not trust what I heard, saw, felt, or experienced. In the past, I've allowed toxic people to enter my life and they took advantage of me.

Evidence against this statement might be: These same people made me feel uneasy and threatened the first time I met them. I had a feeling there was something "off" there, but I didn't listen to what my intuition was telling me. My whole body sensed danger, but I dismissed it as paranoia. There have been many times when I had an intuition I ignored.

Reframing: Although I have been taken advantage of in the past, it doesn't mean I can't trust myself. A lot of my instincts are actually correct, I just haven't followed them because I denied toxic behavior and red flags. Now I know I can trust myself and can make better decisions when I am willing to do so.

Behavior shift: The next time I get a gut feeling about something, I'll try to trust it rather than rationalize, deny, or minimize it. I will listen to what my body is telling me and act accordingly.

Sample Distortion #2: I Can't Say No Because People Would Hate Me

Evidence for: I was punished by authority figures and peers as a child for refusing to comply with their unfair demands. There've been people in my past who decided to walk away from our relationship when I stood up for myself. When I say no, I risk getting reprimanded, pressured, or put down.

Evidence against: I've also had lovely people in my life who respected my wishes and didn't try to coerce or control me when they sensed my discomfort. The people who abandoned me when I stood up for myself ended up being con artists who took advantage of other people.

Reframing: The people who punish me for saying no are exactly the type of boundary-steppers I don't need in my life. Plenty of people are willing to respect my wishes and not push me when they see I am uncomfortable. Standing up for myself and saying no benefits me in the long run, protecting me from exploitative people.

Behavior shift: When someone reacts angrily to my "no" or persistently tries to change my mind, I'll consider it as further evidence that they are toxic. I will limit or cut contact with anyone who tries to do this.

Sample Distortion #3: Everyone Is Doing Their Very Best, I Shouldn't Judge Them

Evidence for: I have known empathic people in the past who made mistakes, including myself. When I asserted myself and called them out on their behaviors, they made changes to improve their behavior.

Evidence against: I have also known plenty of people with long-standing patterns of toxic behavior. Despite expressing how much pain they've caused me, they did not apologize or take any concrete steps to improve their behavior. These people did not try their best. They were looking out for their self-interest.

Reframing: There are empathic people in the world who *are* doing their best and make mistakes. However, I trust myself to know the difference between empathic people like this and toxic people who rarely take responsibility for their destructive behavior. The latter consists of people who don't deserve second chances.

Behavior shift: Rather than applying the platitude of "everyone is just doing their best" to everyone, I will differentiate between people who make mistakes and people who chronically harm me without taking responsibility for their actions. I will implement boundaries and limit contact with the latter group. This isn't about judging people—it's about discerning who they really are. I discern who is healthy for me and who is toxic and will behave accordingly.

A few more examples of reframing distortions can be found in addition to these at http://www.newharbinger.com/45304. There, you will also find the four-step process for reframing so you can practice this method yourself, along with guidance for applying it to the challenge of boosting boundaries, which is a core challenge for HSPs.

Life Skills for Distress Tolerance and Interpersonal Effectiveness

Reframing tools are useful for tackling ingrained thoughts and beliefs that don't serve us well, but HSPs are also in need of concrete strategies for high-conflict social situations that bring up intense emotions, taking a toll on our minds and bodies. The various "life skills" I'll present below to tackle such situations are inspired by dialectical behavior therapy (DBT), an approach developed by Marsha Linehan (2014) that has proven effective for vulnerable populations who struggle with overwhelming emotions.

Life Skill #1: Mindfulness

Mindfulness offers us techniques to remain in the present moment, focusing on one thing at a time. Incorporating the principles of Zen Buddhism, mindfulness prompts us to slow down, breathe through our pain, and use nonjudgment to carefully observe what is happening in our surroundings, describe what we're feeling, and participate more fully in what is occurring.

Mindfulness might look like:

- Taking a five-minute breathing break from a heated conversation and returning to it when you're back to baseline levels of calmness

- Grounding yourself by using your five senses to observe and describe your environment (the sights, smells, sounds) so you don't get overwhelmed in a new social situation

- Returning to the present moment in a social situation by actively listening to what the other person is telling you: noticing their facial expressions, tone of voice, and the environment you're in

- Getting gradually "unstuck" from self-judgmental thoughts to "take in" everything around you

- Noticing your cravings to an addiction or a compulsive behavior, visualizing an "ebb and flow" to your urges as they arise and then pass so you're less likely to act on your emotions impulsively

EXERCISE: **Practicing Mindfulness**

Sit cross-legged in a comfortable position and take long, deep breaths for ten minutes. What sounds, scents, and colors do you notice in your environment? What are you feeling? What thoughts come up? Don't judge your emotions and thoughts, simply imagine them as if they were leaves passing by on a river or words written on a cloud.

Life Skill #2: Emotion Regulation

This life skill reduces vulnerability by tending to our mental and physical well-being. Emotion regulation guides us to appropriately label our emotions and remove obstacles that exacerbate our emotional states. It redirects the HSP to assess what needs are being neglected and what can be done to build positive experiences and take actions to improve the present moment. This skill enables the individual to better manage their emotions, especially in times of adversity.

Emotion regulation might look like:

- Maintaining normal sleep patterns and healthy eating habits to reduce physical vulnerability to stress

- Developing a weekly or daily exercise regimen that gives you a physical outlet for stress, as well as a natural source of mood-lifting endorphins

- Labeling any intense emotions that arise without judgment or resistance—for example, "I am feeling very angry right now"

- Using what is called "opposite action" to deal with overwhelming emotions effectively—for example, when feeling a lot of anxiety, do something soothing like going for a quiet walk by a beautiful river

152

What form of physical exercise do you enjoy the most? Make a plan to work it into your weekly routine.

Life Skill #3: Distress Tolerance and Crisis Management

This skill area focuses primarily on self-soothing, especially during times of crisis, distress, or triggering states of emotional arousal. When managing crises, we can practice radical acceptance, a concept we encountered earlier in the book that promotes neutral acceptance of the present moment and one's emotions within it, without condoning the harmful actions of others or acting impulsively in reaction to unjust adverse circumstances. Surrendering to what is, without condoning it, is not being passive. You can still make changes to your life to improve your circumstances. Accepting is simply about seeing the situation for what it is, not what you want it to be. It gives you space to address the problem rather than adding an extra layer of resistance or denial to it.

Distress tolerance and crisis management might look like:

- Thinking of the pros and cons of a situation to bring about a more balanced perspective—for example, "This man I liked betrayed me. I am so upset, but at the same time, it's a relief to know his true character sooner rather than later. This situation taught me a lot of life lessons and now I don't have to invest in someone who isn't trustworthy."

- Radically accepting a situation for what it is instead of resisting it—for example, "I radically accept that I am getting a divorce. I radically accept my painful emotions. This is what the situation is."

- Self-soothing and improving the moment, with, for example, prayer or visualization (we'll discuss what this looks like more in the section on the VIBRANT acronym later in this chapter)

JOURNAL REFLECTION: **Practicing Radical Acceptance**

What is one situation you can work on radically accepting, without necessarily approving of it? Write down strategies to work through the situation as it is, rather than how you would like it to be.

Life Skill #4: Social Effectiveness

Social effectiveness hones our ability to healthily navigate conflict and social interactions. This life skill plays a crucial role in the mental health of highly sensitive populations because it centers on how to validate ourselves and others when appropriate. It teaches us to appropriately set boundaries and see another's perspective without engaging in black-and-white thinking, all while asserting our needs with confidence and mindfulness.

Social effectiveness might look like:

- Skillfully getting your needs met with a difficult person

- Developing a safety plan to exit unhealthy or dangerous situations with abusers

- Asserting yourself with someone who is receptive to considering your perspective

- Setting boundaries effectively without backing down

JOURNAL REFLECTION: **Practicing Social Effectiveness**

Think about how you can get a need met with one difficult individual in your life.

Two Acronyms to Build HSP Life Skills

As you work to develop the life skills outlined above, a few more acronyms can serve as tools to pave the way for success. The first is CREATES, which will help you get into what therapists call a "wise mind" state to deal more effectively with difficult emotions and situations. Taking these steps cultivates more distress tolerance skills so you can better manage a crisis.

Community

Reprieve

Evaluate progress

Action

Take back control

Enjoyment

Senses

Community. A wonderful way to counteract a crisis is to shift our attention onto two crucial aspects of life: giving back and gratitude. Because HSPs are deeply empathic, contributing to the world makes the most of our gifts and channels our pain into a meaningful purpose. When you're reminded of all the people who are in need and feel gratitude for your own needs that *are* being met, this fortifies your mental health. It redirects your focus *away* from toxic people and onto the greater good of enhancing social connections with people who actually deserve your energy and your giving nature.

You can contribute to your community by donating to a charity, starting a website that spreads awareness about a cause close to your heart, writing a book to help others in adverse circumstances, volunteering, offering to help out a friend or someone who is less privileged—there are countless ways to help improve the world around you and keep your awareness on the bigger picture.

Reprieve. This means temporarily pushing away the situation to obtain emotional distance from it for a short period. To give yourself a reprieve, you can visualize a physical barrier of some kind blocking you from the situation, putting the situation in a "box" temporarily, and refusing to ruminate over it right then. This is definitely not a long-term solution for emotions that have to be dealt with eventually, but it does give you some respite from the pain until you're ready to confront it.

Evaluate progress. When we are in crisis mode and feel as if nothing will ever get better, it's the ideal time to step back and assess. We can evaluate our own progress in life, or we can assess how the circumstances of the crisis we're facing might be less dire than they appear. What someone chooses to evaluate will depend on the particular person and how they react to different types of evaluations. For example, you might get tremendous value from comparing your current life to what it was like ten years ago or comparing your circumstances to someone far less fortunate. You're struggling and in pain now, yes, but things could always be worse.

Some HSPs, however, may feel even more distressed by thinking of unfortunate circumstances, so it would be preferable to evaluate your own or others' success stories instead. When we recall instances of people overcoming similarly adverse situations, we mindfully motivate ourselves to look at the bigger picture and feed the hope that things can get better. We can more clearly see that there are still positive things in our lives *right now.* Find what works for *you* to make you feel better in the moment.

Action. Recall the earlier use of the term "opposite action," when we were discussing the skill of emotion regulation in DBT: engaging in a behavior that is actually the opposite of your current impulse or mood as a means of effectively dealing with the emotion causing you distress. This approach curbs impulsive behavior and positively affects your overall mood by, in essence, flipping to the other side of the coin. This is not about avoidance, which can intensify trauma-related symptoms. Rather, it provides temporary self-soothing for the present moment. If you're feeling particularly angry, for instance, do something calming (like attending a meditation workshop). If you're feeling sad, watch a happy movie or see a comedy show.

Take back control. This step emphasizes the ability to distract yourself from thoughts about the situation and tethering yourself to (nontriggering) activities until you're ready to fully face the present challenge. You can become engrossed in a book, work on a puzzle, or do something creative to anchor you back into a state of control. You can brainstorm small and practical steps to reach out for help and to refocus on what you can change, rather than what is out of your control. For example, if you just suffered a horrendous breakup, taking back control of the situation might look like putting away objects in your home that remind you of your ex and deleting their number from your phone. Removing triggers from your immediate environment reduces the temptation to reach out to the toxic person, who could further hurt you when you're most vulnerable.

Enjoyment. Engaging in distracting pleasurable activities provides temporary relief. Toxic people want us to be focused on our pain and stress, not our pleasure; that's why they work so hard to sabotage our joy—it gives them control. Don't let them have it. Make space for the healthy pleasure you deserve in your life. This will give your mind an enjoyable break from a toxic situation so you can come back later when your body has returned to its normative level of emotional safety. Examples include going for a walk or run, listening to soothing music, turning off your phone, taking a yoga class, going shopping, playing a game, watching a favorite TV show, and engaging in a favorite hobby.

Senses. Put the focus back on your five senses. Common ways to do this include taking very hot or cold showers, holding an ice cube in your hand, snapping a rubber band on your wrist, or any other kind of stimulus that can shake up your senses and distract you from acting impulsively on any destructive urges you may have. Or, if you prefer, you can simply take a moment to mindfully notice all the sights, sounds, smells, and textures in your environment while taking deep breaths. This can be helpful to HSPs who feel especially overwhelmed by sensory input.

JOURNAL REFLECTION:
Apply CREATES to a Challenge You're Facing

Now it's your turn to incorporate this acronym into your life—feel free to work with your therapist, if you have one, to expand upon these suggestions for maximizing the impact of this tool:

- To heighten your sense of **community**, list ten ways you can give back. How would these activities connect to your perceived greater purpose in life? What do they remind you to be grateful for?

- Grant yourself a **reprieve** from the difficult thoughts plaguing you by imagining a barrier that separates you from the situation, giving you space from it. What does it look like?

- Realistically **evaluate progress** you have made in some areas of your life by considering these questions: What are some ways in the past that you successfully dealt with unfortunate situations or some stressful situations that worked out well in the end? Who can you think of who struggled through something similar to what you're facing now and has a success story about it? Are there people you know who are in even more adverse circumstances but who seem to be coping with them well? What do these stories make you appreciate about your own life?

- Take opposite **action** to counteract the negative effects of emotions you're currently experiencing. Write these emotions down, followed by an activity that will elicit the opposite feeling and the improved emotional state you wish to achieve.

- Think of at least one activity you can do right now to help you **take back control** of the situation that is troubling you.

- Find **enjoyment** by taking a pleasure break. What are some activities you can engage in right now to provide that?

- To wake up your **senses**, write down all five of them, and next to each one, list accompanying physical activities that can help jolt you out of your obsessive and ruminating thoughts.

Highly sensitive individuals are prone to experiencing intense emotions, especially in interpersonal situations that are distressing. VIBRANT, the second acronym HSPs can use to learn how to better cope with distress, offers tools you can apply to improve the present moment.

Visualization

Inspiration

Bigger picture

Release

Ask for help

Nourish

Time

Visualization. You can visualize dealing successfully with whatever adverse circumstances you're facing. Imagine escaping to a peaceful place. Brainstorm what it would look like if the situation improved. Any and all of this will slow down catastrophic thinking and allow you to approach the situation with a calmer, collected sense of self.

Inspiration. Motivate and inspire yourself through affirmations, words of encouragement, and positive feedback you've received. Create tangible, visual reminders of these sources of inspiration so you can actually "see" them, like note cards you carry with you, lists you make in your phone, and framed artwork on your desk. Hang a bulletin board containing your favorite affirmations and celebratory pictures; put magnets on your refrigerator of slogans that particularly move you; write yourself a "love letter" with beautiful art or stickers.

Bigger picture. Find meaning in the pain or suffering you're feeling. When we're experiencing intense emotions, we can fall into a sense of learned helplessness. But when we place the focus back on what can be learned from these experiences, we empower ourselves. Rather than saying, "I just had a terrible date—I'm going to be alone forever," reframe the experience: "I just had a terrible date, which has shown me exactly what I don't want in a future relationship. Just another reminder that I deserve the very best and don't have to settle for any less!"

Release. Engage in rejuvenating activities like yoga and meditation to release stressful emotions and to relax and reset your body, especially if it is tense. Trauma tends to get trapped within the body. Yoga and meditation can be useful outlets to "detox" from the impact of negative situations.

Ask for help. Reach out to trustworthy individuals, like your counselor, a close friend, or a compassionate family member. Be open to receiving comfort, validation, and encouragement from others. You can also ask for help from a higher power. Depending on your personal faith and spirituality, you can use prayer to self-soothe, surrender, and seek assistance from the divine. You can also call upon the universe or your higher self for guidance.

Nourish. Mindfully take care of your body and your mind. Eat healthy food, get adequate rest, and choose to consume only positive media sources (avoiding triggering posts on social media, the news, and toxic people during this time of healing). Focus on doing one task at a time to enhance mindfulness. When you're eating a nutritious meal, for example, concentrate on enjoying it rather than pulling out your phone and checking your work email. Nourishing activities remove excessive distractions and reduce the anxiety of dealing with too many emotions at once.

Time. Take the time to calm yourself away from the conflict, whether that means physically removing yourself from a location or mentally distancing yourself for a period of hours, days, or even weeks depending on the situation. Use this time to take a bubble bath, meditate, or walk in nature. Get away for the weekend or spend a whole day with your phone turned off to avoid any triggers or difficult conversations until you're ready to come back to the situation at hand.

JOURNAL REFLECTION:
Apply VIBRANT to a Challenge You're Facing

When you enact this tool to promote self-care strategies in your daily life, your period of detoxification will proceed more smoothly and effectively.

- To practice **visualization**, envision what peace looks like to you. When you're feeling overwhelmed, close your eyes and picture revisiting the most peaceful place you've ever been.

- Find **inspiration** by recalling the best compliments and feedback people have given you. What's the best advice you've received? What's the best advice you've given? Make a poster containing examples of praise and encouragement that you can see every day or record them on your phone to listen to them every morning and night. Say these things to yourself as if you were your own best friend.

- Keep your eye on the **bigger picture** and on growth opportunities by identifying some life lessons you can take away from these experiences. Write down ways to reframe these experiences in a positive light without invalidating the pain you've suffered.

- Get moving to get **release**. List some physical activities you can do immediately to help you release painful emotions and toxic stress.

- You can **ask for help** anytime. What guidance and comfort do you need to hear this very moment?

- Pick one or two activities to **nourish** yourself today without distraction. How will you remove distractions from your environment?

- Where can you go right now to secure a slot of **time** to get a break and create space in which to just be you?

CHAPTER SEVEN

Refuge and Recovery
Healing Modalities for HSPs

Overcoming the traumas of dealing with toxic people takes diverse mind-body techniques to help center ourselves in the present and heal from the past. As I mentioned in the introduction, I've spent most of my life using these techniques to become a more mindful, grounded person who can tackle toxic people with ease. I've also surveyed hundreds of readers on healing modalities, and many of them reported using the activities covered in this chapter to successfully recover from the impact of toxic people.

HSPs can benefit from experimenting with a wide variety of both traditional and alternative remedies to help manage the intensity of our emotions, cope with crisis, and process any traumas that might still be affecting our lives. We'll discuss the options below with a look as to why they work, their benefits, and how to learn more about them. As always, be sure to consult with a therapist to better assess which healing modalities would best suit you and your specific circumstances. There is no "one-size-fits-all" package. These are only suggestions.

Traditional Therapies
Cognitive Behavioral Therapy

Cognitive behavioral therapy (CBT) is a form of psychotherapy that helps us reform maladaptive emotions, behaviors, and thoughts. CBT was developed by Aaron Beck in the 1960s, and research has indicated that it is effective for depression, anxiety disorders, posttraumatic stress disorder, and relationship issues, all of which can be potential struggles for HSPs. Strategies of CBT include identifying cognitive distortions, role-playing to prepare for anticipated conflict, facing one's fears, learning to calm the body during periods of stress, and utilizing problem-solving skills and coping strategies for difficult situations (Clark and Beck 2011).

For HSPs, therapies like CBT can help with identifying cognitive distortions, harmful automatic thoughts, and patterns of behavior related to areas like intimacy, self-esteem, safety, trust, power, and control stemming from interpersonal trauma. These thoughts and beliefs often lead to self-sabotaging behaviors and "manufactured emotions" like misplaced guilt or shame that fuel post-traumatic symptoms. Clients are assisted in challenging and reworking inaccurate beliefs using cognitive restructuring. In doing so, they begin behaving according to healthier and more balanced belief systems regarding themselves, others, and the world.

Other types of therapies that use elements of CBT include cognitive processing therapy (CPT), an evidence-based therapy for those with PTSD symptoms that helps clients identify and work through maladaptive beliefs about trauma and "stuck points" that lead to avoidance behaviors, and prolonged exposure therapy (PET), which helps clients with PTSD become gradually desensitized to trauma-related memories, feelings, and situations.

To learn more about CBT, visit https://beckinstitute.org. For more on CPT and PET, go to https://cptforptsd.com and https://www.apa.org /ptsd-guideline/treatments.

Dialectical Behavior Therapy

Dialectical behavior therapy (DBT) is an evidence-based approach developed by Marsha Linehan, designed to help people who suffer from intense emotions, self-harm, and suicidal ideation. This unique and comprehensive treatment combines Eastern mindfulness techniques with cognitive behavioral methods. As we learned in chapter 6, DBT focuses on four modules: (1) mindfulness; (2) distress tolerance; (3) emotion regulation; and (4) interpersonal effectiveness (McKay, Wood, and Brantley 2010). It is traditionally used for patients with borderline personality disorder (BPD), although, as trauma therapist Arielle Schwartz (2017) notes, many victims with complex PTSD can be misdiagnosed with BPD. Nevertheless, DBT's skills can be used by anyone and everyone.

This form of therapy helps individuals regulate and cope with their emotions, improve their interpersonal effectiveness skills, and stay grounded in the present moment during crises. DBT group therapy sessions allow you to practice and role-play the skills you've learned, providing coping and communication strategies for interactions with difficult people.

As CEO of Psych Central, John M. Grohol, PsyD, says, "DBT theory suggests that some people's arousal levels in such situations can increase far more quickly than the average person's, attain a higher level of emotional stimulation, and take a significant amount of time to return to baseline arousal levels" (2019).

With their high levels of arousal and emotional responsiveness, HSPs may be able to benefit from DBT. Because they become overwhelmed by their environment and social situations, they can use similar skills regarding distress tolerance and emotion regulation to remain calm in situations of high conflict and to implement boundaries effectively. If you also have a history of problems with self-harm, suicidal thoughts, chronic suicide attempts, or extreme and overwhelming emotions, you should consider speaking to a counselor about dialectical behavior therapy. To find a DBT therapist, visit https://behavioraltech .org/resources/find-a-therapist.

Eye Movement Desensitization and Reprocessing

Eye movement desensitization and reprocessing (EMDR) is a form of therapy in which the client is asked to recall traumatic or distressing events while making side-to-side eye movements or using left-to-right hand tapping. It was developed by Francine Shapiro in 1989. Shapiro noticed these eye movements had the effect of alleviating the intense impact of disturbing traumatic memories. EMDR is founded on the theory of adaptive information processing (AIP) which posits that disturbing traumas (including adverse childhood experiences or toxic relationships) are stored in memory in a dysfunctional way and can lead to a maladaptive pattern of thoughts, behaviors and emotions. These traumatic experiences block our normal information-processing mechanism which would allow for natural self-healing and resolution to occur.

Alternating bilateral stimulation such as eye movements or tapping allows this processing to occur freely, encouraging active re-experiencing of the trauma in a space of safety as distressful memories gradually lose their negative charge. As part of its complex eight-phase process, EMDR also identifies negative self-beliefs and beliefs about the world that developed due to the trauma (ex. "I am not lovable" or "The world isn't safe") and locates areas in the body where tension is still stored due to the trauma. The client begins incorporating healthier beliefs to replace these negative associations moving forward; the trauma is then reprocessed in a way that benefits the client. Randomized clinical trials with trauma victims have shown EMDR to be effective for this population. HSPs with adverse childhood experiences can benefit greatly from processing their childhood traumas with an EMDR therapist, to relieve their burden, intensity, and daily impact. To learn more about EMDR and find an EMDR therapist, visit https://www.emdria.org.

Emotional Freedom Techniques

Emotional freedom techniques (EFT) therapy was created by Gary Craig in the 1990s. Much like acupuncture, EFT stimulates energy points on the body, but without the invasive use of needles. These energy points are known as "meridian tapping points," and when tapped, they release trapped energy throughout the body. This is a way to clear our old, destructive feelings and beliefs while replacing them with healthier, positive beliefs.

Coupled with positive affirmations, EFT helps reprogram how we think and feel. Because certain emotions are said to reside in specific parts of the body, EFT allows us to release energetic blocks by allowing electromagnetic energy to flow more freely throughout the body. The affirmations used validate the protective mechanism of negative emotions while allowing clients to feel empowered to let them go. Learn more about EFT at https://eft.mercola.com or read Craig's *EFT Manual* (2011).

Hypnotherapy

Hypnotherapy uses hypnosis to help individuals make behavioral and emotional changes. HSPs can use hypnotherapy to calm their overstimulated nervous system and rework destructive belief systems, conditioning, memories, and wounds that may not otherwise come to conscious awareness. Hypnosis is an altered state of consciousness, a trancelike state in which we are more susceptible to suggestion and therefore able to reprogram our subconscious mind more readily. Hypnosis is also helpful for treating phobias, addictions, chronic pain, and traumatic memories associated with PTSD. Find a qualified hypnotherapist in your area using the Psychology Today search engine at https://www.psychologytoday.com/us/therapists/hypnotherapy.

Group Therapy

Group therapy led by a mental health professional is a safe space to talk about your struggles, fears, and traumas while witnessing others doing the same. This is important because studies show that social support is one of the most important factors in post-trauma recovery (Carlson et al. 2016). You can research groups that focus on domestic violence, trauma, or any other areas you are struggling with at this time. CBT and DBT therapy groups can be excellent places to practice your new skills and engage in constructive role-playing with others. Expressing our emotions with others gives us the validation and support we may have never gotten in toxic relationships, allowing us to access relational healing. It also increases social accountability for maintaining progress and self-care. Search for a therapy group on Psychology Today's search engine at https://groups.psychologytoday.com/rms.

Support Groups

If you struggle with dysfunctional, abusive relationships and have trouble setting boundaries with others, there are support groups that can help validate you and cheerlead your recovery journey. Many survivors have benefited from attending Codependents Anonymous (CoDA) meetings, narcissistic abuse survivor Meetup groups in their local area, and 12-step programs (which can help because you're struggling to "detox" from a narcissistic partner). Search "HSPs" or "empaths" to find groups with people who struggle with high sensitivity just like you.

Nontraditional Supplementary Healing Modalities

Yoga

According to studies, yoga is a powerful and effective complementary treatment for those with PTSD (Kim et al. 2013; Rhodes, Spinazzola, and van der Kolk 2016; Zalta et al. 2018). It helps survivors ease dissociative symptoms, control affective dysregulation, and reduce tension throughout the body. With its powerful reengagement of our bodies, yoga combats the paralysis we experience when we've been traumatized. It increases mindful awareness, allowing individuals to experience "safety and mastery" over their bodies, and gives them the resources to productively interpret intense physiological states when reexperiencing trauma (van der Kolk 2014). This is especially helpful to survivors of physical and sexual abuse and is deeply healing for those recovering from emotional terror.

I personally love hatha yoga and hot vinyasa flow yoga. If you're a beginner, I recommend you take an entry-level class before moving on to more advanced classes. Or, if you struggle with physical injuries, look into restorative yoga.

Meditation

Remember that trauma creates specific changes in the brain, shutting down communication between the more emotional parts of our brain and the frontal lobes that control executive functioning and our ability to organize, plan, think, and make decisions (van der Kolk 2014). It can shrink the hippocampus and hyperactivate the amygdala, areas of the brain that affect emotion, memory, and learning (Morey et al. 2012). Good news: the very areas of the brain that were once affected by trauma can now be rewired by meditation. Research by Harvard neuroscientist Sara Lazar showed that a regular meditation practice for eight weeks can literally change our brain, shrinking the amygdala, which controls the fight-or-flight response, and thickening the hippocampus, which helps with emotion regulation and memory formation (Lazar et al. 2011). Meditation not only strengthens the auditory and sensory parts of our brain, but it also increases gray matter in the frontal lobes, regardless of how old you are.

A forty-minute meditation practice every day can change the way you approach your emotions, your relationships, and your overall sense of happiness. Meditation is free and can be done anywhere at any time. Contrary to popular myth, it doesn't require shutting off your thoughts, but rather observing them, letting them come and go. All you need is a willingness to focus on your breath and a space where you can sit quietly and reflectively.

Be sure to Google and Yelp local meditation centers in your area. Here are some podcasts and channels I follow, some of which are meditation channels and others that are specifically about healing narcissistic abuse. If a link is not provided, you can search for the title on Google or YouTube.

- Meditation Oasis by Mary and Richard Maddux: This is my favorite meditation resource and the one that began my journey. Wonderful for beginners and experts alike. Find it at https://www.meditationoasis.com.

- The Meditation Society of Australia: Download the society's free mp3 meditations at https://download.meditation.org.au.

- YouTube Channels (use search engine):

  - Lucy Rising: Provides meditations specifically for survivors of narcissistic abuse.

  - Yellow Brick Cinema: Offers general relaxing music for meditation.

  - Joseph Clough: International speaker and hypnotherapist Clough offers self-hypnosis meditations and affirmations helpful for retraining the subconscious mind into more positive states.

  - Michael Sealey: Popular YouTuber Michael Sealey provides effective sleep meditations and self-hypnosis for calming anxiety.

Nature

We know that toxic people raise our cortisol (stress) levels. Thankfully, there's a way to counteract that. Scientific research proves nature's ability to lower cortisol levels, relieve stress, improve our ability to concentrate, and lift our mood (Berman, Jonides, and Kaplan 2008; Mayer et al. 2009). Even the act of walking barefoot on the earth during warmer months can improve overall well-being and sleep while reducing pain and stress levels; the theory of the benefits of "earthing" suggests that walking barefoot connects us to the earth's electrons. You can also do this through gardening, which is a very therapeutic and mindful activity that allows you to see the growth you want within manifest externally.

Some ideas for enjoying the daily benefits of nature are: scheduling a morning or an afternoon walk every day; traveling to places with beautiful natural landscapes; taking walks by a river; going to the beach; hiking outdoors; jogging in a park or the woods; and lunching outdoors or picnicking. When the weather is not warm, "access" nature in alternative ways: go camping and start a fire; sit near a fireplace indoors; open the window blinds to let the sunlight in; watch the snow fall; or listen to the rain. Listen to meditation music that incorporates the sounds of rainfall, waterfalls, and ocean waves.

Massage Therapy

Research shows that massage therapy can help lower cortisol levels and boost serotonin and dopamine levels, elevating mood; it also decreases depression, anxiety, irritability, and other trauma-related symptoms (Field et al. 2005; Collinge, Kahn, and Soltysik 2012). These effects are especially potent among populations in need, such as depressed pregnant mothers, those suffering from cancer, and those with migraine headaches. Given this, it's possible that massage therapy can also potentially help with the somatic side effects of trauma. Get creative! Try massages that use hot stones, aromatherapy oils, or even Reiki, in which the practitioner sends you healing energy. Not only will this relieve tension throughout your body, but it also has many mental health benefits.

Not everyone is comfortable being touched by strangers, even a professional. Always take into account your own personal comfort levels and triggers when experimenting with different healing modalities. What works for one HSP may not be right for another.

Journaling and Writing

Trauma literally leaves us speechless, as it deactivates the Broca's area of the brain, the part responsible for communication and speech (van der Kolk 2014). Many traumas become stuck and "frozen" in the nonverbal parts of our brain. Journaling is a way to recommunicate, engaging both the left and the right sides of the brain as we create a more cohesive narrative about the traumas experienced. Researchers discovered that expressive writing improves mood and leads to post-traumatic growth in those with PTSD (Smyth, Hockemeyer, and Tulloch 2008). Track your daily thoughts, emotions, and associated actions in a journal. Share them with your therapist if you have one. It's a helpful way to capture and reflect on common triggers, thought patterns, and behaviors throughout the day.

Affirmations

At graduate school, I researched and interviewed bully victims who used a "resilience narrative" to channel their traumas into professional and personal success. Using positive affirmations to rewrite existing negative narratives is helpful for HSPs who struggle with self-esteem due to their encounters with narcissists and toxic people. Affirmations are a vital part of many of the diverse healing techniques described in this book, and using them is an important way to start healing subconscious wounds by reprogramming how we think about ourselves, our potential, and the world around us.

Affirmations are phrases that help us interrupt our normal thought patterns by instilling positive messages about ourselves and our world. Research confirms that positive affirmations help improve problem solving under stress and that self-affirmations preserve our self-integrity in the face of threat, enabling our "psychological immune system" to defend itself (Creswell et al. 2013; Sherman and Cohen 2006).

For those struggling with low self-esteem, PTSD, or complex PTSD, positive affirmations should be customized in order to prevent triggers. You may have to say affirmations like "I choose to be happy" rather than "I am happy" if you have severe doubts about yourself, to gently and incrementally approach the new beliefs you are working to instill.

Exercise

Those who exercise regularly are less likely to suffer from anxiety and depression (Carek, Laibstain, and Carek 2011). We can replace our biochemical addiction to the chaos and crazy-making of toxic people with healthier alternatives that feed our reward systems and lower our stress levels. When we release endorphins through exercise on a consistent basis, we habituate our bodies to the "drama" of sweating on the treadmill rather than toxic people or bullying peers.

Creating a weekly or even daily exercise regimen is recommended for HSPs. Not only is it a natural mood-lifter, but also research has shown that exercise can potentially improve PTSD symptoms and even curb suicidal ideation among those who are bullied (Fetzner and Asmundson 2014; Sibold et al. 2015). Exercise can also help with overall well-being and coping strategies, giving traumatized individuals a renewed sense of hope and determination, a positive self-image, and an improved quality of life (Caddick and Smith 2017).

Exercise is also a healthy outlet for channeling intense emotions. According to trauma experts, trauma lives in our bodies as well as our minds. Find at least one form of physical release for the intense emotions of grief, rage, and hurt you're bound to feel in the aftermath of abuse and trauma, in order to combat the paralysis that accompanies trauma, leaving us feeling numb and frozen.

I personally love kickboxing, yoga, dance, cardio, and running while listening to empowering music or positive affirmations. Do something you're passionate about and love to do. Don't force your body into activities that you're not comfortable with or exhaust yourself. Even a daily ten-minute walk in nature can be more helpful than staying sedentary, so do the best you can and don't overexert yourself. Using physical exercise as an outlet should be an act of self-care, not self-destruction or negative self-talk.

Laughter Therapy

According to medical researcher Lee Berk (1989), grief induces stress hormones like cortisol which suppress your immune system. On the other hand, laughter lowers these hormones and gets feel-good neurochemicals like dopamine flowing. Laughter can also ease pain and enhance overall well-being, providing numerous health benefits. HSPs should take advantage of the healing benefits of laughter. Laughter yoga, for example, incorporates the use of voluntary laughter to reap the same benefits. Take time each day to make yourself laugh. You can watch stand-up comedy on Netflix, browse through silly Instagram meme accounts, attend an improv show, recall funny memories, watch funny videos or movies, or read amusing books or stories. Stick to what makes *you* laugh—everyone's sense of humor and personal preferences are different, so find something that uniquely tickles your funny bone.

Aromatherapy

Aromatherapy is an alternative healing method whereby the individual uses scents and essential oils as a way to help with emotions and health. Individuals can choose to inhale the fragrance or apply the diluted oils directly on their skin. According to certified massage therapist and cranial sacral therapist Suzanne Bovenizer (2017), our sense of smell is connected to the limbic system in our brain, where emotions and memories are stored. Scents stimulate that part of the brain, releasing chemicals that cause us to become calmer and more relaxed. Aromatherapy can help a great deal with anxiety, which can be a key component of the distress victims of narcissistic abuse experience.

You can buy essential oils and an essential oil diffuser for your home so that aromatherapy is always accessible to you. You may also seek aromatherapy in alternative ways: some yoga centers offer yoga with an aromatherapy component, and many massages also incorporate elements of aromatherapy into sessions.

I recommend both essential oils and incense. Here are some recommendations for aromatherapy (searchable on Amazon):

- Artizen Aromatherapy Top 14 Essential Oil Set

- URPOWER Essential Oil Diffuser

- Aromatherapy Incense Sticks: Certified Organic and All Natural Essential Oils

- *The Complete Book of Essential Oils and Aromatherapy* by Valerie Ann Worwood

Acupuncture

In "Stories of Healing Emotional Trauma in My Acupuncture Clinic," licensed acupuncturist Nicholas Sieben (2013) writes, "According to Chinese Medical theory, trauma lives in our bodies. It becomes stuck in our blood and bones where it incubates, causing various physical and mental symptoms. To fully resolve trauma, the body needs to be released. There needs to be a physical detox."

Acupuncture is an ancient Chinese healing technique involving the use of needles at specific points of the body to heal a wide variety of physical and psychological ailments. There are twelve primary and eight secondary invisible lines of energy flow in the body known as "meridians." An acupuncturist targets specific points of the body to help resolve the physical and/or emotional ailment plaguing the patient. To learn more about acupuncture, visit https://nccih.nih.gov/health /acupuncture/introduction. If you live in the United States, you can also search for an acupuncturist at https://www.nccaom.org/find-a -practitioner-directory.

Animal-Assisted Intervention

Perhaps we didn't receive support for our highly sensitive natures from humans, but animals provide us with unconditional love and approval. A systematic review of research on animal-assisted intervention (AAI) and how it helps survivors of child abuse and military veterans found that the use of AAI as a complementary treatment for trauma was effective for reducing depression, PTSD symptoms, and anxiety (O'Haire, Guérin, and Kirkham 2015). This will come as no surprise to any survivor who's engaged in a little bit of pet therapy, whether it be playing with dogs, horses, cats, bunnies, or birds.

According to Marguerite O'Haire and her colleagues, "With respect to intrusion, the presence of an animal is purported to act as a comforting reminder that danger is no longer present and to act as a secure base for mindful experiences in the present." Those who suffer from PTSD often experience a sense of emotional numbness, but animals can evoke positive emotions and serve as "social facilitators," which helps us reduce loneliness and isolation. In addition, contact with animals can boost our oxytocin levels naturally, providing a healthier source of this feel-good hormone without involving toxic people.

Music Therapy

Music can regulate our mood, reconnect us with our authentic emotions, reduce our heart rate and blood pressure, lower stress, and manage our anxiety levels. Music can even be used in a therapeutic relationship to help addicts in their recovery, improve social functioning in patients with schizophrenia, and reduce the side effects of cancer treatment.

You can learn about music therapy with a licensed practitioner at https://www.musictherapy.org. In terms of using music as a self-care tool, HSPs may have special needs when it comes to the music they listen to. Soothing, calming music can help their already overstimulated nervous systems. However, even HSPs have "power songs"—songs that energize them, immediately lift their spirits, and motivate them to tackle the day. Make a list of songs that make you feel empowered, calm, relaxed, and energetic. Then make it a habit of listening to music every day to center yourself and reconnect with your joy.

Self-Care MEDICINE

In order to maintain this level of self-care throughout your life as an HSP, use the acronym MEDICINE to reduce your emotional vulnerability. This tool contains many helpful reminders for HSPs, who may neglect their health when they're consumed by overwhelming emotions and by the impact of toxic relationships.

Medicinal support

Eating mindfully

Drug avoidance

Intellect

Caretaking

Idolize

Nurse injuries and triggers

Exercise

Medicinal support. People who struggle with the effects of trauma often experience a greater severity and frequency of health problems and medical conditions; this can be due to the long-term activation of biological stress pathways, like their HPA axis over-releasing the stress hormone cortisol during the fight or flight response, which decreases immune activity (Pacella, Hruska, and Delahanty 2013). Take care of any illnesses or ailments that make you feel physically taxed or distressed.

JOURNAL REFLECTION: **Medical Inventory**

List any medical or mental health conditions you have that require proper care and treatment. Beneath each condition, write down medications and the contact information for any therapists, support groups, or doctors you can call whenever you're experiencing difficulty with this condition.

Write down any factors that worsen these conditions and ways to prevent aggravating them. This helps preemptively address problems and escalations before they begin.

Eating mindfully. Our minds cannot recover from toxic people when our bodies are depleted of the nutrients they require to be at their optimal state. Eat in a nourishing, healthful manner that benefits your overall well-being. Work with a nutritionist to find a healthy meal plan tailored toward you and your body's unique needs. Examples include incorporating a daily green juice or increasing your vegetable and fruit intake, cutting out excessive dairy or caffeine assumption, and drinking plenty of water throughout the day to remain hydrated.

JOURNAL REFLECTION: **Healthy Habits**

What do you think is healthy about your current eating habits? What would you like to improve? What is one new, healthy dietary habit you can introduce into your daily routine? Examples: using raw cacao powder and stevia in your desserts instead of sugar; replacing starches with low-carb alternatives like cauliflower, healthy fats, and other vegetables; substituting red meat with lean protein like chicken; and swapping out creamer for almond milk in your coffee each morning.

Drug avoidance. Encountering toxic people can cause us to "numb" ourselves through the use of drugs, alcohol, or even excessive caffeine and sugar to get a temporary fix. Avoid mood-altering drugs unless you have a prescription. Alcohol and excessive caffeine can hinder your recovery from emotional inundation and may even cause more problems.

JOURNAL REFLECTION: **Overstimulating Drugs**

Are there any drugs you're abusing for which you want to receive treatment? How often do you use caffeine or alcohol to improve your mood?

What alternatives can help you wean off of excessive use of caffeine or alcohol (examples: herbal tea, exercise, beverages with lower alcoholic content, flavored water)?

Intellect. Take care of your mind—it's just as important to evaluate what you consume mentally as physically. What kinds of ideas and beliefs are you feeding your mind every day? If you have a lot of negative self-talk, it can help to work with a counselor and track these thoughts in a journal, to reflect and challenge these patterns.

What are you allowing to rent space in your mind? Are you reading traumatic books, watching horror films, looking at an abusive ex-partner's social media, or revisiting texts from a toxic ex-friend? If so, limit or obliterate these types of activities from your schedule. Block that ex from all your social media, balance your television consumption by adding comedy or lighthearted movies to the mix, and read books that focus on solutions rather than problems. You can also replace any sort of toxic consumption with more mood-lifting media, such as soothing meditation audio recordings or videos of adorable animals.

If you're having trouble focusing throughout the day, track your sleep patterns and any negative thinking patterns that may be disrupting your mind. Getting enough rest and establishing a regular sleep schedule is important so that your brain can process information throughout the day and not become overwhelmed.

JOURNAL REFLECTION: **What Are You Consuming?**

Which social media platforms do you follow, and how healthy are they? How many hours of sleep do you get every night? How often do you feel sluggish? Are there ways to improve your sleeping environment to make it a more soothing, relaxing place? Consider listening to calming music before bed, changing your bedroom walls or furniture to softer colors, lighting candles instead of bright lights to alleviate eye strain, and using memory foam pillows.

Caretaking. It's important to check in with yourself throughout the day to ensure that you are getting everything you need. This is *especially* important in the aftermath of a breakup with a toxic person, because you are now shifting from being their caretaker and confidant to your own. Treat yourself as if you were your own caretaker and enlist the support of other loved ones to help care for you when needed.

JOURNAL REFLECTION: **Taking Care of Your Own Needs**

As a caretaker, treat yourself with self-compassion by asking, "What do I need right now? Do I need to eat? Sleep? Take a shower? Call a friend?" Then follow through accordingly.

Idolize. A lot of us HSPs idolize *others* and forget to extend that same honor to ourselves. When we make toxic people God-like in our life, we neglect our own divinity. Feed your spirit by giving yourself encouragement, praise, and compassionate attention. Honor yourself and revere the divinity within yourself.

According to self-help author Louise Hay (2016), mirror work can be a great way to do this. Every morning, you can stare into your eyes in the mirror and compliment yourself. Say, "I love you. I adore you. You are precious. You are worthy. You are valuable." Alternatively, if you believe in God or a higher power, you can also say affirmations like, "God loves me. I am a child of God. I know everything is going to be all right because the universe always takes care of me." Whatever form your affirmations take is totally okay—they can be customized to best suit your needs and spiritual beliefs. Feed yourself joyful affirmations and remember that your beautiful spirit transcends just your physical form. This kind of positive self-talk can do wonders for your self-esteem if you make it a daily habit.

EXERCISE: **Mirror Work**

Look in the mirror. What encouraging affirmations can you say to your-self? What parts of yourself do you love and accept? Toward which per-ceived flaws can you send approval and self-compassion?

Nurse injuries and triggers. Tend to existing injuries so that they will heal properly and prevent anything from exacerbating these wounds—and we're not talking about just physical hurts here. Preemptively take an inventory of all potentially triggering situations in your life and actively prevent them from escalating. For example, unfriend someone on Facebook who has been writing offensive posts or avoid the route where your ex-partner lives on your way to school. Schedule an extra counseling session with a therapist in times of high emotional distress. Or, rather than taking your usual train to work, opt for a peaceful cab ride when you know it's going to be a particularly stressful day and you want to start the morning off right. Measures like these "cushion the blow" so that existing triggers don't get further inflamed before you've had time to process them.

JOURNAL REFLECTION: **Trigger Management**

Write down a list of ten triggers and ways to avoid or lessen their impact.

Exercise. Getting enough fresh air and exercise every day can release endorphins, lift your mood, and help keep you in a balanced emotional state even in times of extreme duress—all of which makes exercise the ideal stress reliever when you're dealing with a toxic person. A daily exercise regimen can also help you feel more confident when you're challenged to assert yourself against bullies and exploiters.

JOURNAL REFLECTION: **Endorphin Boost**

How often do you exercise per week? Per day? Is there an easy and convenient form of exercise you can do for at least thirty minutes each day (examples: walk around the neighborhood, go for a bike ride, dance to a choreography video)? How can you balance getting exercise outdoors and indoors?

Many healing modalities are available to you as an HSP, and all of those presented above have been used effectively by people just like you. Your goal is to find what works for *you* and your unique needs. Experiment with alternative and traditional approaches. It's recommended you consult a therapist before you try any modality that might be triggering for you. The important thing for you to remember is that self-care is a vital part of the journey to becoming a more empowered HSP and healing from the impact of toxic people.

HSPs who are equipped with the tools to tackle conflict, engage in self-care, and deal effectively with toxic individuals can become empowered superheroes. You are now aware of how our highly sensitive personalities make us natural targets for emotional predators. You have become well versed in the manipulation tactics of narcissistic and toxic personalities and have examined the addictive nature of relationships with these types. Now you can be on the lookout.

I hope this book has not only helped you understand the mind-sets and behaviors of toxic people, but that it has also equipped you with the tips and resources needed to effectively navigate them with more confidence and appreciation for your high sensitivity. Remember, the world needs HSPs like you—those who can use their superpowers for the greater good and their highest good. But you can't save anyone until you first learn to save and honor yourself.

Acknowledgments

Thank you to all my beautiful readers for their incredible support since I first began writing about this topic in 2014 and to the courageous survivors who shared their stories with me. A special thank you to my hardworking parents, Rehana and Mohammed, who worked tirelessly to ensure that their children could achieve their dreams in America. I'm grateful for my sister, Tania, who has always supported my dreams as a writer. Thank you to the many terrific professors and mentors who've shaped my writing and academic development over the years: Laura Polan, Dr. John Archer, Dr. Aaron Pallas, Dr. Holly Parker, Dr. Maureen McLane, Dr. Hope Leichter, Dr. Sarah Kleiman, Dr. James Uleman, Dr. Ellsworth Fersch, Dr. Elizabeth Malouf, Louise Lasson, LCSW, Dr. Ronald Corbett, and Dr. Karen Adolph. Thanks to James Zika, Terry Powell, and Angela Garcia for supporting my professional development.

My infinite gratitude to the amazing Andrea Schneider, LCSW, for vetting this book and for her priceless encouragement. I can't thank fellow advocates enough for their generous support: Jackson MacKenzie; Pete Walker, MFT; Dr. Athena Staik; Dr. John Grohol; Dr. Annie Kaszina; Monica White, LMHC; Kristin Sunanta Walker; Lisa A. Romano; Kim Saeed; Melanie Vann, MA; Kris Godinez, LPC; and many other powerful truth-tellers. Thank you to Thought Catalog, which gave me a platform for my voice and for my writing to be shared with millions, and to Psych Central for spreading my message.

Finally, I am eternally grateful to the gifted New Harbinger team and its editors for bringing this book to life: Jess O'Brien, who approached me with this wonderful opportunity and always blew me away with his kindness; Jennifer Holder, who diligently ensured that my voice shined through effectively to readers; Cindy Nixon, who went above and beyond to brilliantly polish this book; and everyone who contributed to this guide.

References

Acevedo, B. P., E. N. Aron, A. Aron, M. Sangster, N. Collins, and L. L. Brown. 2014. "The Highly Sensitive Brain: An fMRI Study of Sensory Processing Sensitivity and Response to Others' Emotions." *Brain and Behavior* 4(4): 580–594.

APA (American Psychiatric Association). 2013. *Diagnostic and Statistical Manual of Mental Disorders*. 5th ed. Arlington, VA: American Psychiatric Publishing.

Archer, D. 2017. "The Danger of Manipulative Love-Bombing in a Relationship." *Psychology Today*, March 6. Accessed January 26, 2019. https://www.psychologytoday.com/us/blog/reading-between-the-headlines/201703/the-danger-manipulative-love-bombing-in-relationship.

Aron, A., E. Melinat, E. N. Aron, R. D. Vallone, and R. J. Bator. 1997. "The Experimental Generation of Interpersonal Closeness: A Procedure and Some Preliminary Findings." *Personality and Social Psychology Bulletin* 23(4): 363–377.

Aron, E. 2016. *The Highly Sensitive Person: How to Thrive When the World Overwhelms You*. New York: Harmony Books.

Bartels A., and S. Zeki. 2000. "The Neural Basis of Romantic Love." *NeuroReport* 11(17): 3829–3834.

Baumeister, R. F., E. Bratslavsky, C. Finkenauer, and K. D. Vohs. 2001. "Bad Is Stronger Than Good." *Review of General Psychology* 5(4): 323–370.

Baumgartner, T., M. Heinrichs, A. Vonlanthen, U. Fischbacher, and E. Fehr. 2008. "Oxytocin Shapes the Neural Circuitry of Trust and Trust Adaptation in Humans." *Neuron* 58(4): 639–650.

Begg, I. M., A. Anas, and S. Farinacci. 1992. "Dissociation of Processes in Belief: Source Recollection, Statement Familiarity, and the Illusion of Truth." *Journal of Experimental Psychology: General* 121(4): 446–458.

Bergland, C. 2013. "Cortisol: Why the 'Stress Hormone' Is Public Enemy No. 1." *Psychology Today*, January 22. https://www.psychologytoday.com/blog/the-athletes-way/201301/cortisol-why-the-stress-hormone-is-public-enemy-no-1.

Berk, L. S., S. A. Tan, W. F. Fry, B. K. Napier, J. W. Lee, R. W. Hubbard, J. E. Lewis, and W. C. Eby. 1989. "Neuroendocrine and Stress Hormone Changes During Mirthful Laughter." *The American Journal of the Medical Sciences*, 298(6): 390-396.

Berman, M. G., J. Jonides, and S. Kaplan. 2008. "The Cognitive Benefits of Interacting with Nature." *Psychological Science* 19: 1207–1212.

Bonchay, B. 2017. "Narcissistic Abuse Affects Over 158 Million People in the U.S." PyschCentral.com, May 24. Accessed October 12, 2018. https://psychcentral.com/lib/narcissistic-abuse-affects-over-158 -million-people-in-the-u-s.

Bovenizer, S. 2017. "The Limbic System." Accessed July 1, 2019. https:// suebovenizer.com/the-limbic-system.

Bowen, S., N. Chawla, S. E. Collins, K. Witkiewitz, S. Hsu, J. Grow, S. Clifasefi et al. 2009. "Mindfulness-Based Relapse Prevention for Substance Use Disorders: A Pilot Efficacy Trial." *Substance Abuse* 30(4): 295–305.

Brach, T. 2020. *Radical Compassion: Learning to Love Yourself and Your World with the Practice of RAIN.* London: Rider Books.

Bradshaw, J. 1990. *Homecoming: Reclaiming and Championing Your Inner Child.* London: Piatkus.

Brummelman, E., S. Thomaes, S. A. Nelemans, B. O. Castro, G. Overbeek, and B. J. Bushman. 2015. "Origins of Narcissism in Children." *Proceedings of the National Academy of Sciences* 112(12): 3659–3662.

Buttafuoco, M. J., and J. McCarron, J. 2009. *Getting It Through My Thick Skull: Why I Stayed, What I Learned, and What Millions of People Involved with Sociopaths Need to Know.* Deerfield Beach, FL: Health Communications.

Caddick, N., and B. Smith. 2017. "Combat Surfers: A Narrative Study of Veterans, Surfing, and War Trauma." *Movimento* 23(1): 35.

Carek, P. J., S. E. Laibstain, and S. M. Carek. 2011. "Exercise for the Treatment of Depression and Anxiety." *International Journal of Psychiatry in Medicine* 41(1): 15–28.

Carlson B., P. A. Palmieri, N. P. Field, C. J, Dalenberg, K. S. Macia, K. S., and D. A. Spain. 2016. "Contributions of Risk and Protective Factors to Prediction of Psychological Symptoms After Traumatic Experiences." *Comprehensive Psychiatry*, 69: 106-115.

Carnell, S. 2012. "Bad Boys, Bad Brains." *Psychology Today*, May 14. https://www.psychologytoday.com/blog/bad-appetite/201205/bad-boys -bad-brains.

Carnes, P. P. 2015. *Betrayal Bond: Breaking Free of Exploitive Relationships.* Deerfield Beach, FL: Health Communications.

Carter, S. B. 2012. "Emotions Are Contagious—Choose Your Company Wisely." *Psychology Today,* October 20. Accessed October 12, 2018. https://www.psychologytoday.com/us/blog/high-octane-women /201210 /emotions-are-contagious-choose-your-company-wisely.

Carver, J. 2014. "Stockholm Syndrome: The Psychological Mystery of Loving an Abuser." CounsellingResource.com, December 20. Accessed February 28, 2019. https://counsellingresource.com/therapy /self-help/stockholm/2/.

Cascio, C. N., M. B. O'Donnell, F. J. Tinney, M. D. Lieberman, S. E. Taylor, V. J. Strecher, and E. B. Falk. 2015. "Self-Affirmation Activates Brain Systems Associated with Self-Related Processing and Reward and Is Reinforced by Future Orientation." *Social Cognitive and Affective Neuroscience* 11(4): 621–629.

Clark, A., and A. T. Beck. 2011. *Cognitive Therapy of Anxiety Disorders: Science and Practice.* New York: Guilford Press.

Collinge, W., J. Kahn, and R. Soltysik. 2012. "Promoting Reintegration of National Guard Veterans and Their Partners Using a Self-Directed Program of Integrative Therapies: A Pilot Study." *Military Medicine* 177(12): 1477–1485.

Craig, A. D. 2009. "How Do You Feel—Now? The Anterior Insula and Human Awareness." *Nature Reviews Neuroscience* 10(1): 59–70.

Craig, G. 2011. *The EFT Manual.* Santa Rosa, CA: Energy Psychology Press.

Creswell, J. D., J. M. Dutcher, W. M. Klein, P. R. Harris, and J. M. Levine. 2013. "Self-Affirmation Improves Problem-Solving Under Stress." *PLoS ONE* 8(5).

De Becker, G. 2010. *The Gift of Fear: Survival Signals That Protect Us from Violence.* London: Bloomsbury.

Drexler, S. M., C. J. Merz, T. C. Hamacher-Dang, M. Tegenthoff, and O. T. Wolf. 2015. "Effects of Cortisol on Reconsolidation of Reactivated Fear Memories." *Neuropsychopharmacology* 40(13): 3036–3043.

Durvasula, R. 2018. "Narcissist, Psychopath, or Sociopath: How to Spot the Differences." Medcircle.com, August 8. Accessed October 9, 2018. https://www.youtube.com/watch?v=6dv8zJiggBs.

Dutton, D. G., and A. P. Aron. 1974. "Some Evidence for Heightened Sexual Attraction Under Conditions of High Anxiety." *Journal of Personality and Social Psychology* 30(4): 510–517.

Elliott, S. 2009. *Getting Past Your Breakup: How to Turn a Devastating Loss into the Best Thing That Ever Happened to You.* Cambridge, MA: Da Capo Lifelong.

Felitti, V. J., R. F. Anda, D. Nordenberg, D. F. Williamson, A. M. Spitz, V. Edwards, M. P. Koss, and J. S. Marks. 1998. "Relationship of Childhood Abuse and Household Dysfunction to Many of the Leading Causes of Death in Adults." *American Journal of Preventive Medicine* 14(4): 245–258.

Ferster, C. B., and B. F. Skinner. 1957. *Schedules of Reinforcement.* New York: Appleton-Century-Crofts.

Fetzner, M. G., and G. J. Asmundson. 2014. "Aerobic Exercise Reduces Symptoms of Posttraumatic Stress Disorder: A Randomized Controlled Trial." *Cognitive Behaviour Therapy* 44(4): 301–313.

Field, T., M. Hernandez-Reif, M. Diego, S. Schanberg, and C. Kuhn. 2005. "Cortisol Decreases and Serotonin and Dopamine Increase Following Massage Therapy." *International Journal of Neuroscience* 115(10): 1397–1413.

Fisher, H. E. 2016. "Love Is Like Cocaine." *Nautilus,* February 4. http:// nautil.us/issue/33/attraction/love-is-like-cocaine.

Fowler, J. S., N. D. Volkow, C. A. Kassed, and L. Chang. 2007. "Imaging the Addicted Human Brain." *Science & Practice Perspectives* 3(2): 4–16.

Geraci, L., and S. Rajaram. 2016. "The Illusory Truth Effect: The Distinctiveness Effect in Explicit and Implicit Memory." *Distinctiveness and Memory,* 210–234.

Glenn, A. L., and A. Raine. 2014. *Psychopathy: An introduction to biological findings and their implications.* New York: New York University Press.

Gottman, J. M. 1994. *Why Marriages Succeed or Fail: And How You Can Make Your Marriage Last.* New York: Simon & Schuster.

Goulston, M. 2012. "Rage—Coming Soon from a Narcissist Near You." *Psychology Today,* February 9. Accessed February 11, 2019. https:// www.psychologytoday.com/us/blog/just-listen/201202/rage-coming -soon-narcissist-near-you.

Greene, R. 2004. *The Art of Seduction.* Eastbourne, UK: Gardners Books.

Grohol, J. 2019. "An Overview of Dialectical Behavior Therapy." PsychCentral.com, June 19. Accessed February 9, 2020. https:// psych central.com/lib/an-overview-of-dialectical-behavior-therapy.

Gudjonsson, G. H., and J. F. Sigurdsson. 2003. "The Relationship of Compliance with Coping Strategies and Self-Esteem." *European Journal of Psychological Assessment* 19(2): 117–123.

Handlin, L., M. Petersson, and K. Uvnäs-Moberg. 2015. "Self-Soothing Behaviors with Particular Reference to Oxytocin Release Induced by Non-noxious Sensory Stimulation." *Frontiers in Psychology* 5: 1529.

Hasher, L., D. Goldstein, and T. Toppino. 1977. "Frequency and the Conference of Referential Validity." *Journal of Verbal Learning and Verbal Behavior* 16(1): 107–112.

Hatfield, E., J. T. Cacioppo, and R. L. Rapson. 2003. *Emotional Contagion.* Cambridge, UK: Cambridge University Press.

Hay, L. L. 2016. *Mirror Work: 21 Days to Heal Your Life.* Carlsbad, CA: Hay House.

Herdieckerhoff, E. 2016. "The Gentle Power of Highly Sensitive People." Speech presented at TEDxIHEParis, Paris, November. https://www .youtube.com/watch?v=pi4JOlMSWjo.

Impett, E. A., A. Kogan, T. English, O. John, C. Oveis, A. M. Gordon, and D. Keltner. 2012. "Suppression Sours Sacrifice." *Personality and Social Psychology Bulletin* 38(6): 707–720.

Jagiellowicz, J., X. Xu, A. Aron, E. Aron, G. Cao, T. Feng, and X. Weng. 2011. "The Trait of Sensory Processing Sensitivity and Neural Responses to Changes in Visual Scenes." *Social Cognitive and Affective Neuroscience* 6(1): 38–47.

Jiang, H., M. P. White, M. D. Greicius, L. C. Waelde, and D. Spiegel. 2017. "Brain Activity and Functional Connectivity Associated with Hypnosis." *Cerebral Cortex* 27(8): 4083–4093.

Kaiser, P., D. Kohen, M. Brown, R. Kajander, and A. Barnes. 2018. "Integrating Pediatric Hypnosis with Complementary Modalities: Clinical Perspectives on Personalized Treatment." *Children* 5(8): 108.

Kernberg, O. F. 1984. *Severe Personality Disorders: Psychotherapeutic Strategies.* New Haven, CT: Yale University Press.

Kim, H., S. M. Schneider, L. Kravitz, C. Mermier, and M. R. Burge. 2013. "Mind-Body Practices for Posttraumatic Stress Disorder." *Journal of Investigative Medicine* 61(5): 827–834.

Kimonis, E. R., P.J. Frick, E. Cauffman, A. Goldweber, and J. Skeem. 2012. "Primary and Secondary Variants of Juvenile Psychopathy Differ in Emotional Processing." *Development and Psychopathology,* 24(3): 1091–1103.

Klein, S. 2013. "Adrenaline, Cortisol, Norepinephrine: The Three Major Stress Hormones, Explained." HuffPost.com, April 19. http://www .huffingtonpost.com/2013/04/19/adrenaline-cortisol-stress-hormones _n_3112800.html.

Korb, A. 2011. "Boosting Your Serotonin Activity." *Psychology Today*, November 17. Accessed July 1, 2019. https://www.psychologytoday.com /us/blog/prefrontal-nudity/201111/boosting-your-serotonin-activity.

Kuster, M., S. Backes, V. Brandstätter, F. W. Nussbeck, T. N. Bradbury, D. Sutter-Stickel, and G. Bodenmann. 2017. "Approach-Avoidance Goals and Relationship Problems, Communication of Stress, and Dyadic Coping in Couples." *Motivation and Emotion* 41(5): 576–590.

Lange, J., D.L. Paulhus, and J. Crusius. 2017. "Elucidating the Dark Side of Envy: Distinctive links of benign and malicious envy with dark personalities." *Personality and Social Psychology Bulletin*, 44(4): 601-614.

Lazar, S. W., J. Carmody, M. Vangel, C. Congleton, S. M. Yerramsetti, T. Gard, and B. K. Hölzel. 2011. "Mindfulness Practice Leads to Increases in Regional Brain Gray Matter Density." *Psychiatry Research: Neuroimaging* 191(1): 36–43.

Linehan, M. M. 2014. *DBT Skills Training Manual.* New York: Guilford Press.

MacDonald, M., and S. Sherry. 2016. "N.S. Research Lays Out How to Recognize Narcissistic Perfectionists." CTV News, April 22. Accessed February 9, 2020. https://www.ctvnews.ca/lifestyle/n-s-research-lays -out-how-to-recognize-narcissistic-perfectionists-1.2870230.

Marazziti, D., H. S. Akiskal, A. Rossi, and G. B. Cassano. 1999. "Alteration of the Platelet Serotonin Transporter in Romantic Love." *Psychological Medicine* 29(3): 741–745.

Marsh, J., and V. Ramachandran. 2012. "Do Mirror Neurons Give Us Empathy?" *Greater Good*, March 29. Accessed October 12, 2018. https://greatergood.berkeley.edu/article/item/do_mirror_neurons _give_empathy.

Martinez-Lewi, L. 2018. "Are You Married to a Jekyll Hyde Covert Narcissist?" December 5. Accessed June 23, 2019. http://thenarcissist inyourlife.com/are-you-married-to-a-jekyll-hyde-covert-narcissist.

Mayer, F. S., C. M. P. Frantz, E. Bruehlman-Senecal, and K. Doliver. 2009. "Why Is Nature Beneficial? The Role of Connectedness in Nature." *Environment and Behavior* 41: 607–643.

McKay, M., J. C. Wood, and J. Brantley. 2010. *The Dialectical Behavior Therapy Skills Workbook: Practical DBT Exercises for Learning*

Mindfulness, Interpersonal Effectiveness, Emotion Regulation & Distress Tolerance. Oakland, CA: New Harbinger Publications.

Mikkelsen, K., L. Stojanovska, and V. Apostolopoulos. 2016. "The Effects of Vitamin B in Depression." *Current Medicinal Chemistry* 23(38): 4317–4337.

Mogilski, J. K., and L. L. Welling. 2017. "Staying Friends with an Ex: Sex and Dark Personality Traits Predict Motivations for Post-Relationship Friendship." *Personality and Individual Differences* 115: 114–119.

Morey, A., A. L. Gold, K. S. Labar, S. K. Beall, V. M. Brown, C. C. Haswell, J. D. Nasser et al. 2012. "Amygdala Volume Changes in Posttraumatic Stress Disorder in a Large Case-Controlled Veterans Group." *Archives of General Psychiatry* 69(11): 1169.

Motzkin, J. C., J. P. Newman, K. A. Kiehl, and M. Koenigs. 2011. "Reduced Prefrontal Connectivity in Psychopathy." *Journal of Neuroscience* 31(48): 17348–17357.

National Domestic Violence Hotline. 2018. "Why We Don't Recommend Couples Counseling for Abusive Relationships." February 18. Accessed October 9, 2018. https://www.thehotline.org/2014/08/01/why-we-dont -recommend-couples-counseling-for-abusive-relationships.

Navarro, J. 2017. *Dangerous Personalities: An FBI Profiler Shows How to Identify and Protect Yourself from Harmful People.* Emmaus, PA: Rodale.

Neff, K. 2011. "The Chemicals of Care: How Self-Compassion Manifests in Our Bodies." HuffPost.com, August 27. Accessed February 8, 2020. https://www.huffpost.com/entry/self-compassion_b_884665.

Newberg, A. B., and M. R. Waldman. 2013. *Words Can Change Your Brain: 12 Conversation Strategies to Build Trust, Resolve Conflict, and Increase Intimacy.* New York: Plume.

Odendaal, J., and R. Meintjes. 2003. "Neurophysiological Correlates of Affiliative Behaviour Between Humans and Dogs." *Veterinary Journal* 165(3): 296–301.

O'Haire, M. E., N. A. Guérin, and A. C. Kirkham. 2015. "Animal-Assisted Intervention for Trauma: A Systematic Literature Review." *Frontiers in Psychology* 6: 2.

Olds, J., and P. Milner. 1954. "Positive Reinforcement Produced by Electrical Stimulation of Septal Area and Other Regions of Rat Brain." *Journal of Comparative and Physiological Psychology* 47(6): 419–427.

Orloff, J. 2018. *The Empath's Survival Guide: Life Strategies for Sensitive People.* Boulder, CO: Sounds True.

Pacella L., B. Hruska, and D.L. Delahanty. 2013. "The Physical Health Consequences of PTSD and PTSD Symptoms: A meta-analytic review. *Journal of Anxiety Disorders*, 27(1): 33–46.

Palgi, S., E. Klein, and S. G. Shamay-Tsoory. 2016. "Oxytocin Improves Compassion Toward Women Among Patients with PTSD." *Psychoneuroendocrinology* 64: 143–149.

Pipe, J. 2014. "Stonewalling vs. Empathy." May 1. Accessed February 28, 2019. http://tapestryassociates.com/stonewalling-vs-empathy.

Reis, H. T., S. M. Smith, C. L. Carmichael, P. A. Caprariello, F. Tsai, A. Rodrigues, and M. R. Maniaci. 2010. "Are You Happy for Me? How Sharing Positive Events with Others Provides Personal and Interpersonal Benefits." *Journal of Personality and Social Psychology* 99(2): 311–329.

Rhodes, A., J. Spinazzola, and B. van der Kolk. 2016. "Yoga for Adult Women with Chronic PTSD: A Long-Term Follow-Up Study." *Journal of Alternative and Complementary Medicine* 22(3): 189–196.

Rockliff, H., P. Gilbert, K. McEwan, S. Lightman, and D. Glover. 2008. "A Pilot Exploration of Heart Rate Variability and Salivary Cortisol Responses to Compassion-Focused Imagery." *Clinical Neuropsychiatry* 5(3): 132–139.

Sarkis, S. 2017. "Are Gaslighters Aware of What They Do?" *Psychology Today*, January 30. Accessed February 16, 2020. https://www .psychologytoday.com/us/blog/here-there-and-everywhere/201701 /are-gaslighters-aware-what-they-do.

Schrodt, P., P. L. Witt, and J. R. Shimkowski. 2013. "A Meta-Analytical Review of the Demand/Withdraw Pattern of Interaction and Its Associations with Individual, Relational, and Communicative Outcomes." *Communication Monographs* 81(1): 28–58.

Schulze, L., I. Dziobek, A. Vater, H. R. Heekeren, M. Bajbouj, B. Renneberg, B. Heuser, and S. Roepke. 2013. "Gray Matter Abnormalities in Patients with Narcissistic Personality Disorder." *Journal of Psychiatric Research* 47(10): 1363–1369.

Schwartz, A. 2017. *The Complex PTSD Workbook: A Mind-Body Approach to Regaining Emotional Control and Becoming Whole*. Berkeley, CA: Althea Press.

Sherman, D. K., and G. L. Cohen. 2006. "The Psychology of Self-Defense: Self-Affirmation Theory." *Advances in Experimental Social Psychology* 38: 183–242.

Sibold, J., E. Edwards, D. Murray-Close, and J. J. Hudziak. 2015. "Physical Activity, Sadness, and Suicidality in Bullied US Adolescents." *Journal of the American Academy of Child & Adolescent Psychiatry* 54(10): 808–815.

Sieben, N. 2013. "Stories of Healing Emotional Trauma in My Acupuncture Clinic." NicholasSieben.com, January 30. Accessed February 7, 2020. https://nicholassieben.com/stories-of-healing-emotional-trauma-in-my -acupuncture-clinic.

Simon, G. 2018. "Personalities Prone to Narcissistic Manipulation." January 13. Accessed October 12, 2018. https://www.drgeorgesimon .com/personalities-prone-to-narcissistic-manipulation.

Smyth, J. M., J. R. Hockemeyer, and H. Tulloch. 2008. "Expressive Writing and Post-Traumatic Stress Disorder: Effects on Trauma Symptoms, Mood States, and Cortisol Reactivity." *British Journal of Health Psychology* 13(1): 85–93.

Stein, T. 2016. "Narcissist or Sociopath? Similarities, Differences and Signs." *Psychology Today*, August 11. Accessed October 14, 2018. https:// www.psychologytoday.com/us/blog/the-integrationist/201608/narcissist -or-sociopath-similarities-differences-and-signs.

Stern, R. 2007. *The Gaslight Effect: How to Spot and Survive the Hidden Manipulations Other People Use to Control Your Life*. New York: Morgan Road Books.

Stout, M. 2005. *The Sociopath Next Door: The Ruthless Versus the Rest of Us*. New York: Broadway Books.

Suomi, S. J. 2011. "Risk, Resilience, and Gene-Environment Interplay in Primates." *Journal of the Canadian Academy of Child and Adolescent Psychiatry* 20(4): 289–297.

Tatar, J. R., E. Cauffman, E.R. Kimonis, and J. L. Skeem. 2012. "Victimization History and Posttraumatic Stress: An analysis of psychopathy variants in male juvenile offenders." *Journal of Child & Adolescent Trauma*, 5(2): 102–113

Tourjée, D. 2016. "Narcissists and Psychopaths Love to Stay Friends with Their Exes." Vice.com, May 10. Accessed August 10, 2018. https:// broadly.vice.com/en_us/article/ezjy3m/narcissists-and-psychopaths-love -to-stay-friends-with-their-exes.

Walker, P. 2013. *Complex PTSD: From Surviving to Thriving*. Lafayette, CA: Azure Coyote.

Walster, E. 1965. "The Effect of Self-Esteem on Romantic Liking." *Journal of Experimental Social Psychology* 1(2): 184–197.

Wang, D. V., and J. Z. Tsien. 2011. "Convergent Processing of Both Positive and Negative Motivational Signals by the VTA Dopamine Neuronal Populations." *PLoS ONE* 6(2).

Warshaw, C., E. Lyon, P. J. Bland, H. Phillips, and M. Hooper. 2014. "Mental Health and Substance Use Coercion Surveys: Report from the National Center on Domestic Violence, Trauma & Mental Health and the National Domestic Violence Hotline."

Watson, R. 2013. "Oxytocin: The Love and Trust Hormone Can Be Deceptive." *Psychology Today*, October 14. https://www.psychology today.com/blog/love-and-gratitude/201310/oxytocin-the-love-and-trust -hormone-can-be-deceptive.

Westbrook, C., J. D. Creswell, G. Tabibnia, E. Julson, H. Kober, and H. A. Tindle. 2011. "Mindful Attention Reduces Neural and Self-Reported Cue-Induced Craving in Smokers." *Social Cognitive and Affective Neuroscience* 8(1): 73–84.

Williams, K. D., and S. A. Nida. 2011. "Ostracism." *Current Directions in Psychological Science* 20(2): 71–75.

Van der Kolk, B. 2014. *The Body Keeps the Score: Brain, Mind, and Body in the Healing of Trauma.* New York: Viking.

Zalta, A. K., P. Held, D. L. Smith, B. J. Klassen, A. M. Lofgreen, P. S. Normand, M. B. Brennan et al. 2018. "Evaluating Patterns and Predictors of Symptom Change During a Three-Week Intensive Outpatient Treatment for Veterans with PTSD." *BMC Psychiatry* 18(1): 242.

Zwolinski, R. 2014. "The Silent Treatment and What You Can Do to Stop It Cold." PsychCentral.com, November 18. Accessed February 28, 2019. https://blogs.psychcentral.com/therapy-soup/2014/11/the-silent-treatment-and-what-you-can-do-to-stop-it-cold.

Shahida Arabi, MA, is a summa cum laude graduate of Columbia University, and best-selling author of three books, including *Becoming the Narcissist's Nightmare* and *Power*. Her work has been featured on *Psychology Today*, *Psych Central*, *Salon*, *HuffPost*, *Bustle*, the National Domestic Violence Hotline, the New York *Daily News*, *Thought Catalog*, and VICE Media Group. Find out more about her at www.shahidaarabi.com.

Foreword writer **Andrea Schneider, LCSW**, is a licensed clinical social worker in the San Francisco Bay Area, and has over twenty years of experience counseling thousands of individuals and families. She specializes in narcissistic abuse recovery, maternal wellness, trauma recovery, special needs parenting, grief, and loss. You can find out more about her at www.andreaschneiderlcsw.com.

MORE BOOKS from
NEW HARBINGER PUBLICATIONS

**THE MIND-BODY
STRESS RESET**

Somatic Practices to
Reduce Overwhelm &
Increase Well-Being

978-1684034277 / US $17.95

**DISARMING THE
NARCISSIST,
SECOND EDITION**

Surviving & Thriving with
the Self-Absorbed

978-1608827602 / US $17.95

**ENERGY HEALING
FOR EMPATHS**

How to Protect Yourself from
Energy Vampires, Honor
Your Boundaries & Build
Healthier Relationships

978-1684035922 / US $21.95

ⓇREVEAL PRESS
An Imprint of New Harbinger Publications

**THE ASSERTIVENESS
GUIDE FOR WOMEN**

How to Communicate Your
Needs, Set Healthy Boundaries,
& Transform Your Relationships

978-1626253377 / US $16.95

**THE HIGHLY
SENSITIVE PERSON'S
SURVIVAL GUIDE**

Essential Skills for Living Well
in an Overstimulating World

978-1572243965 / US $18.95

**ADULT CHILDREN OF
EMOTIONALLY
IMMATURE PARENTS**

How to Heal from Distant,
Rejecting, or Self-Involved Parents

978-1626251700 / US $18.95

🌢 **newharbinger**publications
1-800-748-6273 / newharbinger.com

(VISA, MC, AMEX / prices subject to change without notice)
Follow Us 🔲 f 🔲 🔲 🔲 in

Don't miss out on new books in the subjects that interest you.
Sign up for our **Book Alerts** at **newharbinger.com/bookalerts** 🖱

Register your **new harbinger** titles for additional benefits!

When you register your **new harbinger** title—purchased in any format, from any source—you get access to benefits like the following:

- Downloadable accessories like printable worksheets and extra content

- Instructional videos and audio files

- Information about updates, corrections, and new editions

Not every title has accessories, but we're adding new material all the time.

Access free accessories in 3 easy steps:

1. Sign in at NewHarbinger.com (or **register** to create an account).

2. Click on **register a book**. Search for your title and click the **register** button when it appears.

3. Click on the **book cover or title** to go to its details page. Click on **accessories** to view and access files.

That's all there is to it!

If you need help, visit:

NewHarbinger.com/accessories

new harbinger
CELEBRATING
40 YEARS